PURE GOLDIE

PURE GOLDIE

The Life and Career of Goldie Hawn

Marc Shapiro

A Birch Lane Press Book
Published by Carol Publishing Group

A Birch Lane Press Book
Published by Carol Publishing Group
Birch Lane Press is a registered trademark of Carol Communications, Inc.

Editorial, sales and distribution, rights and permissions inquiries should be
addressed to Carol Publishing Group, 120 Enterprise Avenue, Secaucus, N.J.
07094.

In Canada: Canadian Manda Group, One Atlantic Avenue, Suite 105, Toronto,
Ontario, M6K 3E7

Carol Publishing Group books may be purchased in bulk at special discounts for
sales promotion, fund-raising, or educational purposes. Special editions can be
created to specifications. For details, contact Special Sales Department, Carol
Publishing Group, 120 Enterprise Avenue, Secaucus, N.J. 07094.

Manufactured in the United States of America
10 9 8 7 6 5 4 3 2 1

Library of Congress Cataloging-in-Publication Data

Shapiro, Marc.
    Pure Goldie : the life and career of Goldie Hawn / by Marc
Shapiro.
        p.   cm.
    "A Birch Lane Press book."
    Filmography: p.
    Includes bibliographical references and index.
    ISBN 1–55972–467–6 (hc)
    1. Hawn, Goldie.   2. Motion picture actors and actresses—United
States—Biography.   I. Title.
PN2287.H334S52   1998
791.43′028′092—dc21
    [B]   98–3268
                                                             CIP

Contents

Acknowledgments

My wife, Nancy. Love is love. My daughter, Rachael. For the good times. Selma. Hi, Mom! Bennie and Freda. How is the air up there? Lori. The best agent on the planet. The good people at Carol Publishing Group. Charles Bukowski, Patti Smith, Edgar Allan Poe, Kiss, and Black Sabbath, who occupy the best part of the dark side. And, finally, thanks, Goldie. For the laughs and the tears.

Introduction: Why Goldie?

A book on the life and times of Goldie Hawn. Well, okay. But why?

As perceived by the public, Goldie Hawn is essentially a one-trick pony. She is exceptional at one thing, comedy. However, once you get beyond the laughs, there is more to Goldie than meets the eye.

It took conviction and persistence of the highest order in 1980 for Goldie Hawn to demand that she not only star in but produce the movie *Private Benjamin*. At a time when you could count the number of women with clout in Hollywood on one hand and still have a couple of fingers left, Goldie's bravery and pioneering spirit in bucking the "old-boy" Hollywood system took guts. But her reputation was not assured with the success of *Private Benjamin*. In the ensuing years, she would constantly battle, sometimes quietly, sometimes aggressively, for more power and in the process kick open the door for the next generation of female filmmakers and prove over and over again that the Goldie Hawn we all grew to love on *Laugh-In* was a character and not the reality.

And the reality for this consummate actress, powerhouse producer, and rising directorial power, capable of topflight performances in any kind of vehicle, is that her success has not been a slam dunk.

There's a reason why Goldie won an Oscar for *Cactus Flower* in 1969. And it comes as no surprise that she drew raves for the likes of *Private Benjamin, The First Wives' Club,* and of course, *Laugh-In*. Her sense of comic timing and her physical presence were beyond reproach. But she has also been prone to caricature and playing down to the stereotype that has grown up around her, which is why Goldie has such throwaway efforts as *Wildcats, Overboard,* and *HouseSitter* on the downside of her career ledger.

Comedy? Let's say she's batting .300. Enough to keep her in the major leagues but not enough for her to bat cleanup on a consistent basis.

Drama? *The Girl From Petrovka. Deceived. Crisscross.* Once again the baseball analogy comes into play. Does the phrase "Good hit but no field" ring a bell?

So what makes Goldie Hawn somebody we want to read about? She's got talent, she's got guts, and perhaps most importantly, when it comes to pure, unadulterated humanity, there is not a soul in Hollywood that can touch her.

Goldie Hawn is somebody everybody likes. It's always sunny, never cloudy, when Goldie's around. She could be an actress, a housewife, a typist in the steno pool, a meter maid, or a hooker. Happy would always be part of the package. That you did not know her from Adam would not matter. What would is that you would have this uncontrollable urge to run up to Goldie and hug her and have the feeling that you would get quite a heartfelt hug in return.

Because being real is not an act for Goldie Hawn. It's a way of life.

Get on her good side and you're likely to be invited over to her house for dinner. Get on her bad side and in a quietly forceful way you'll be shown the door. It is that kind of honesty that has endeared the actress to those who have followed her personal and professional life.

I don't know about anyone else, but when Gus Trikonis and Bill Hudson, Hawn's two ex-husbands, dragged her through the dirt that is divorce court, I wanted to kick their collective butts! Why? Because Goldie was just too good a person to be treated that way. And when Goldie won the Oscar for *Cactus Flower,* I was thrilled for her, even though I really did not think much of the movie.

Guys could easily see getting a chance at Goldie Hawn, taking her home to mother or to bed (if only Kurt Russell had not gotten there first). Hell! Most guys would settle for just being friends. Women see Hawn as that eternal high school best friend, the one they could shop or dish the dirt with. You could tell Goldie anything and be sure that it would go no further.

But there is more to Goldie Hawn than sheer likability. It is easy to relate to somebody who, occupation aside, has had an "everyperson" kind of life. The Goldie Hawn odyssey has been filled with the kinds of small triumphs and big disasters that we all go through.

When she talks about how tough it was dancing on tabletops in New Jersey—well, we all know what it can be like working for "the man" every day. Hitting it big on *Laugh-In,* was like matching numbers on a lottery ticket. If rushing home after a hard day's work, hoping against hope that she would not be too late to tuck her children into bed, does not hit home in our "there's never enough hours in the day" world, nothing can.

Goldie has had personal problems that could not be solved by all the money and fame in the world. So have we all. She did not feel sorry for herself. She dealt with them and then moved on.

Goldie has qualities we would like to think we possess. Spirit, drive, emotion, the ability to love and hate. When I look at most of the reigning supersisters of Tinseltown, I have a hard time seeing a soul behind the Hollywood veneer. I don't have that problem with Goldie.

And so, finally, that's why a book on Goldie Hawn. Because real people like to read about real people. And in the best sense of the term, Goldie Hawn is just plain folks.

PURE GOLDIE

1

Go Figure

GOLDIE HAWN NEVER WANTED MUCH OUT OF LIFE. "ALL I EVER wanted to do was run a dance school and marry a Jewish dentist," the actress said in examining her early hopes and dreams.

Fortunately, the gods had bigger things in store.

Hawn walked into a society party late in 1996, resplendent in a shocking red slip dress that accentuated a body that belied her fifty-one years. Not that age was a factor for the actress, who had long ago acknowledged that her days as an ingenue had already come and gone. She was comfortable with that fact of life and had quite effortlessly made the transition from dizzy cutie-pie to mature leading lady.

As partygoers greeted her and engaged in high-society small talk, the old Goldie Hawn magically appeared. Her eyes were wide, and a sparkle seemed to radiate from them. That full, toothy, little-girl, shy smile, which had been a constant as far back as her *Laugh-In* days, was much in evidence.

This sudden reemergence of the familiar Goldie was in stark contrast to Hawn's appearance months earlier, at the premiere of *The First Wives' Club*. Hawn, holding tightly to the arm of longtime love Kurt Russell as they walked down the red carpet, was visibly nervous and uncomfortable—a surprising emotion considering that advance word of mouth on her first full-blown starring vehicle in years had been overwhelmingly positive. But then nobody could blame Hawn for, emotionally, taking baby steps.

Following the death of her mother in 1993, Hawn had remained largely low profile, spending quality time with her family and only gradually easing back into her career. She finally resurfaced in 1995 as Woody Allen's ex-wife in the screwball musical comedy *Everybody Says I Love You* (which ended up, typical of Woody Allen productions, gathering much advance word of mouth preceding an eventual 1996 release). The film had received generally favorable notices and, according to Hawn, had been a fairly good testing of the waters. She had gotten on famously with one of the most notoriously temperamental filmmakers in the business and shown that the years off had only resulted in a renewed sense of desire to be in front of the camera, strutting her stuff.

But *The First Wives' Club* was a whole other animal. The project, despite starring Hawn, Diane Keaton, and Bette Midler, was considered a risk in Hollywood. Women's stories, and especially women's revenge stories, were like boxcars with one six already showing. Despite the film's all-star cast, Hawn could not hide. She would be out front for the first time in a long while. Even knowing that Hollywood was forgiving, especially of actresses with her track record, Goldie had her fingers crossed very tightly as the film's first images flickered onto the big screen.

Close to $100 million in box-office receipts later, the consensus, was by those who air-kissed and hugged the actress at the party, that Goldie Hawn was back. Not that she had ever really been away. For hers is a star that has always shined in the Hollywood universe. Sometimes flickering and fading; at other times, glowing bright. But always most definitely there.

One could see that there was something special as far back as her fluffy breakout role in television's *Laugh-In*, as a Hollywood stereotype of bubbleheadedness that she effectively sent up and just as quickly left behind with notable performances in *Cactus Flower, There's a Girl in My Soup, The Sugarland Express, $* (Dollars), and

Shampoo. Sharp-eyed critics could see the depth of talent that had already begun to emerge.

Hawn has always been big on instinct throughout her career, taking roles for no other reason than that they seemed right at the time and constantly waging war against the stereotype that has continued to dog her. And when you take risks, you sometimes get burned. Just look at Goldie's acting resumé: a crapshoot of career choices in which Hawn mixed above-average films in the late 1960s and early 1970s, like the bittersweet love story *The Girl From Petrovka* and the heartwarming *Butterflies Are Free*, with uncharacteristically mediocre choices in the 1980s, like the star-driven but ultimately lackluster *Best Friends* and *Bird on a Wire*.

"You don't hit a home run every time," quipped Hawn when looking back on the mixed bag that has been her career. "Some things just worked out, and some didn't."

Hawn was speaking professionally. But it should come as no surprise that her personal life has also been a start-and-stop work in progress.

The actress's early marriage to choreographer and aspiring film director Gus Trikonis cost her financially and emotionally in the end. A little older and a little wiser, she married again, this time to entertainer Bill Hudson, and though the ride was less bumpy, the result was unhappily the same. Hawn, whose frothy exterior has always concealed a sharp and concise mind, would often fall back on platitudes and clichés, citing career conflicts and time spent apart, to explain her failed marriages. But with the years have come a certain reality.

"I used to say that it doesn't matter who makes the money in a marriage," she stated as a bottom line to her troubled relationships, "but I was obviously very naive at the time. Because it did matter."

When it came time to choose yet another life partner, Hawn, in her gathered wisdom and slightly unorthodox approach to life, picked Kurt Russell, an established actor who would take the emotional pressure of being the sole breadwinner off her shoulders. For fifteen years they have shown that love and commitment can survive in the absence of a legal contract. Hawn, who recently described Russell as her "lover for life," has been adamant in talking about how this nontraditional relationship has been "no accident."

"I've been consistently happy for years, and that's due to meeting the right man and the tremendous freedom we allow each other," the actress said, reflecting on the relationship with Russell that began in 1982. "I call Kurt my husband, and he calls me his wife. We're not living in sin. We're living in love."

After four decades in Hollywood, with seemingly nothing left to prove, and after fielding the inevitable flood of scripts following the success of *The First Wives' Club* but finding nothing to get excited about, Hawn stepped into the fire once again. Having already proved herself as an actress and a producer, this time she took on the role of director. Her chosen debut project was a TNT movie for television called *Hope,* which chronicles a teenage girl's coming-of-age in the shadow of the atomic bomb and in a racially explosive time. It was a risk that Goldie Hawn need not have taken, but it comes as no surprise that she did.

"Life sort of unfolds, and certain things, which you can't plan, reveal themselves at the right time," Hawn reflected. "I realized here was a chance to exert influence."

And Hawn, comfortable and excited with this resurgence, is showing no signs of letting down. She is currently weighing the possibility of costarring with Steve Martin in the remake of the classic film *The Out of Towners.* Also on the drawing board is a costarring role, opposite Madonna, in the movie version of the hit musical *Chicago* and the screen version of the Larry McMurtry novel *The Desert Rose,* which she has designs on directing. Also high on her development list as another starring-directing vehicle is the highly personal *Ashes to Ashes,* in which a woman takes her dead husband's ashes to India.

"There are certain stories that I want to tell, and there are certain stories that I feel should be told," she said of her fuller-than-full plate. "Having influence makes these things possible."

It also has not hurt the actress in her decades-long odyssey toward freedom and happiness that she has managed the unthinkable by Hollywood standards: She has not made any long-lasting enemies.

Conflicts that typically end up giving the highest-profile celebrities bad reputations seem to roll off her like water off a duck's back. Despite a bitter legal struggle with Hawn after the star terminated his services, former manager Art Simon never thought it necessary to blast his former client. Neither has first husband Gus Trikonis, who, after a protracted and quite ugly divorce proceeding, made some early evenhanded comments to the press about what he perceived as the reality of their relationship but steadfastly refused to trash his ex-wife.

The reason for Goldie's "good as gold" reputation is that she refuses to carry a grudge even when it would be justified. Not that Goldie has never fired back at an adversary. When ex-husband Bill Hudson knocked her for denying regular visitation rights, Goldie proved, in a number of public statements to the press, that she could get down in the dirt with the best of them. But Goldie's thing, with rare exception, is to put people in their place without raising a ruckus. And nowhere was this more evident than at a February 1996 awards ceremony when Hawn became the first actress ever honored by the American Museum of Moving Image.

On that night, Hawn, arm in arm with Russell, walked into the gala and was immediately surrounded by well-wishers. Russell, knowing it was Goldie's night, drifted a few feet away, unselfishly allowing Goldie's big night to be totally hers. There were the expected hugs and kisses from guests and, in particular, the attention of a rather oily studio executive who shall go unnamed.

He hugged Goldie and then lingered to talk, all the while his hand resting on her hip. As they continued to talk, the executive's hand began moving slowly but surely toward Goldie's behind. It was obvious to many that the dirty old man was attempting to cop a feel. Goldie, continuing to smile, appeared either to not have a clue or was choosing to ignore his unwanted attentions. Russell was standing only fifteen feet away. If he turned and noticed, would he go ballistic? Would Goldie's day of glory turn into one of embarrassment?

Goldie suddenly took the executive's groping hand in hers, held it warmly in front of her for all to see, smiled, and walked away. Everyone who witnessed the incident knew that it was Goldie's way of showing him up for the slime he was. Everybody, that is, except the executive, who was left standing alone in the reception area. He apparently did not have a clue that he had just been put down, Goldie style.

It is Goldie Hawn's response to life—meeting it head-on, dealing with it in the most subtle way possible, and moving on—that has made her the best kind of survivor. One with beauty, brains, and the will to advance through life on her own terms. It's no wonder that Goldie Hawn, even when she's been down, has not been down for very long.

While basking in the glow of her *First Wives' Club* success, Hawn recently joked about her "alleged" comeback. "Yeah, I'm back"—she laughed, attempting a halfhearted gruff voice—"and I'm bad." Bad, in a constantly moving, constantly spirited approach to life and love? Yes, one could believe that. But being back? That's a bit off base.

Because Goldie Hawn never really left.

2

Happy Days...Sort Of

GOLDIE HAWN WAS NOT THE FIRST MEMBER OF HER FAMILY TO BE underestimated.

Her ancestor Edward Rutledge, the youngest signer of the Declaration of Independence, was dismissed by future president John Adams as "a peacock" and "excessively vain and weak" in the early chaotic days of the American War of Independence. But Rutledge ultimately proved to be more than a Yankee Doodle Dandy, establishing himself as a first-rate fighter in the American Revolution, an influential lawmaker as a member of the South Carolina legislature, and, later, a governor of that state in the years following the break from England.

The times were equally turbulent and no less exciting when musician Edward Rutledge Hawn, a WASP from Arkansas, met, courted, and eventually married Laura Speinhoff, a Jewish jewelry wholesaler from Pittsburgh during the onset of the Great Depression in October 1929. There were some rumblings in both families about the interfaith nature of the marriage. On Laura's side there was trepidation about her marrying into the unstable world of a professional musician.

But Edward and Laura Hawn were made of stern stuff. There was no lack of confidence that the married couple would make a good life for themselves, even if it meant moving to a place they'd never been before.

"Daddy moved to Washington, D.C., with my mother during the Depression," said Hawn of her family odyssey. "Washington was a good town for musicians during the 1930s because there was plenty of work to be found playing state banquets and government functions."

But not necessarily enough work to make a living and establish a solid foundation for the family they knew they would someday have. So the Hawns immediately began burning the candle at both ends.

By day they ran a jewelry store and watch-repair shop. Then it was home to a quick dinner, a quick nap, and Edward would be off to spend the night playing, depending on the job, the violin, clarinet, or sax in any pickup band with a chair to fill.

The hard work eventually paid off, and the Hawns prospered. They moved to a white Tudor duplex in the suburb of Takoma Park, Maryland.

Laura Hawn became pregnant in 1936 and gave birth to a daughter, Patti, in 1937. The next seven years saw even more professional growth for the Hawn family. Edward had come to be much in demand as a musician and was making inroads into the higher-profile orchestras in the D.C. area. Laura, exercising her long-held interest in dance, had entered into a partnership with a like-minded area instructor and opened a local dance studio, the Roberta Fera School of Dance. Everybody appeared happy except Patti, who was chafing at the idea of being an only child.

"It all started when I realized I was the only kid on the block who didn't have a brother or sister," related the elder sibling of the events that led to the birth of Goldie. "It was embarrassing. All the other kids had stories to tell, and I was jealous. So I nudged my parents and then just stayed out of their bedroom long enough until they had Goldie."

Goldie Jeanne Hawn (named after her mother's maternal grandmother) was born on November 21, 1945, into a nontraditional home whose liberal leanings allowed for the celebration of both Hanukkah and Christmas and whose spoken and unspoken encouragement set Goldie on the right emotional path. Years later, Hawn would remember those years as "emotionally supportive and geared toward an assertive kind of life." From the moment she entered the world, Hawn gave the impression, to her family, of being a happy child.

"When I came out of my mother's vagina"—Goldie chuckled when reminded of those first impressions of her—"God went 'Bing! You're going to be happy, and you're going to pass that happiness around.'"

The Hawn household was, from Goldie's earliest memories, an exciting place to be. Music was a constant, as was dance. Hawn, with childish enthusiasm, was quick to latch on to the idea of a life in the world of entertainment. At age three, she managed to figure out enough chords on the family piano to play "Happy Birthday." And while you could not tell much about Hawn's inclination, let alone talent, as a toddler, her mother knew "absolutely" that showbiz was in tiny Goldie's future and that it was not too early to start.

"It was not originally my decision," said the candid Hawn of her mother's determination, when Goldie was three, to enroll her and her sister in the Roberta Fera School of Dance. "But I kind of liked the idea that my mom saw me as another Ginger Rogers."

Laura Hawn would chauffeur her children to classes in tap and ballet three to five times a week and watch proudly as Goldie and Patti limbered up and then gracefully executed their ballet routines. Both Hawn girls enjoyed the process, but in Laura's mind Goldie was showcasing something extra. "I really enjoyed it," remembered Goldie "and even though I was quite young, dance became just another part of my life that I would always look forward to."

Laura Hawn's thrusting of her daughters into the limelight at an early age would seem like a classic case of stage-mothering. But in later years Goldie vehemently denied that her mother was acting out of anything but positive motives. "She wasn't a stage mother or anything like that. It's just that she knew me. I was never forced. But she would always say, 'If you learn to dance, Goldie, it will open doors for you.'"

Hawn's mother echoed the notion that she only had Goldie's best interests at heart when she introduced her barely-out-of-diapers daughter to the possibilities of dance. "I introduced the idea and encouraged her. But Goldie responded to the experience very positively. If she had not, I would not have forced her."

Hawn's life away from dance was a nurturing, trauma-free experience in which Edward and Laura Hawn parceled out equal doses of discipline and love. "Dad was a dreamer, and Mom was a pragmatist," reflected Patti Hawn. "Goldie and I are a mixture of both."

And for Goldie the strong feeling of family was an early, comforting feeling. "I had two parents. There was never a fear of them splitting up. We had dinner on the table at six o'clock. Every night. They were very consistent, which is what children need, and I know it affected me in a very positive, loving manner. I can remember almost all of my childhood," she continued, "and all of my memories are pleasant. There was no conflict, no push, and no competition in my family."

And this stable family life resulted in Goldie's developing an affectionate and open nature during those early years. Hawn, in reflecting back on her childhood, beamed at the memory of "being the little girl who loved to kiss everybody good night." She also remembered the impromptu living-room dance recitals and skits with her sister that would inevitably bring the laughs and applause that were music to the young girls' ears. Hawn's mother, who was often the sole audience for Goldie's performances, jokingly related that "Goldie was the type of girl who would always put on her tutu and dance whether you wanted her to or not."

Sister Patti soon realized that while they both had "a natural affinity for dance," Goldie was the one who was serious about it. "While she was discovering pirouettes and arabesques, I was discovering boys." And Patti laughingly recalled that once she discovered boys, their age difference produced the inevitable conflicts. "That was about the time I started dreaming of a lock on my bedroom door to keep Goldie out of my stuff. She would play with my makeup, my shoes, and my jewelry. To this day I'm not sure if she actually got into my diary."

What Patti is sure of is that her dates were often kick-started by embarrassing encounters with her younger sister. "My dates usually began awkwardly, mostly because of Goldie. Because she's a born mimic, I could always count on her to ruin my entrances, especially when I first started wearing high heels. My date would be waiting downstairs, and I would come down trying to keep my balance and my cool. Goldie would follow behind me, imitating my wobble, and my date would double up with laughter."

But there was more to Goldie's early years than being a pain in the neck and an entertainer in training. Her outgoing performing persona was balanced by a sensitive side prone to introspection. Goldie, in later years, would regularly refer back to those moments spent alone. "My growing-up years in Takoma Park were so wonderful. I have so many great memories, and a lot of those have to do with nature. Picking flowers by the creek, going off and finding little hideouts, or just lying back and looking up at the clouds. Those are the kinds of memories that own your heart forever."

Laura Hawn was a loving mentor, always encouraging Goldie to move to the next emotional plateau but always there with an ever-ready shoulder to cry on. "I'm a lot like my mother," recalled Goldie of the attitudes ingrained in her by her mother. "She was extremely hooked in to her family, and she always worked. There was never any question that my sister and I would have to go out and earn a living. And we never thought that a man would support us."

What the young Hawn found in her father, Edward, was a parent quick with sage advice and guidance and somebody who could be memorable and quotable. "My father always kept me on the straight and narrow in terms of what was real and what wasn't," recalled Hawn of those inevitable talks in their living room and at the kitchen table. "He said, 'If you think you're too big for your britches, just go stand in the ocean and feel how small you really are.' He also told me, 'Always look like you know where you're going. If you need me, the umbilical chord is stretching wherever you are. Don't pick your nose in public, and put the butter back in the icebox.' I always remember that kind of stuff."

Elementary school years continued to be a happy, if less than

13

noteworthy time for Hawn. Dance had been supplemented by lessons in voice, piano, and acting, and, before the age of ten, Goldie got her first real taste of the spotlight when she danced with the chorus of a local production of *The Nutcracker Suite* with the famed Ballet Russe de Monte Carlo. For her portrayal of Clara in her first professional job, Hawn received a check for $1.50.

Goldie's talents soon became well known within the Hawn family circle, and the young girl would eagerly respond to requests for impromptu dance and piano recitals. Hawn related that a particular request to entertain at a friend's bar mitzvah, at age twelve, brought home certain realities. The young Goldie had come to expect a certain degree of proficiency from herself, and so she was a little flustered at the bar mitzvah when she fell only moments into the dance routine. Goldie got up, started the routine again and just as quickly fell again. Finally, on a third attempt, she was the graceful Goldie Hawn people had come to expect. "I learned an important lesson that day. I realized that if I kept at it, I was probably the little girl who was going to make it."

But before she would begin the odyssey of making it, Hawn had to endure the terrors of adolescence. Goldie had already come to grips with the fact that she "was not a pretty child. I had very large eyes and a full mouth. I really hated those things about me." Consequently, by the time she reached junior high school and with a full schedule that included swimming, cheerleading, and dance as well as her normal studies, Goldie was insecure about her looks and just about everything else.

Goldie tended to make friends fairly easily, which eased her introduction into the terrible teens. But in recalling that time, Goldie presented a not-too-flattering portrait of a young girl filled with self-doubt, resulting primarily from her perception of herself as totally unattractive.

Hawn's mother, in a diplomatic bit of understatement, indicated that "Goldie's teen years were a difficult time for her. She was a late bloomer who was not quite as physically developed as the other girls." Goldie, in a painful bit of self-examination, was more critical.

14

"I went through this period when I really felt inadequate. I was very flat-chested. I had absolutely no shape. My ankles were thin, and I'd have to wear petticoats to make my hips look bigger."

Young Goldie's self-image was so bad that it began to affect her attitude toward dancing. She would complain about how lessons were getting to be a drag and at one point, at age thirteen, announced to her parents that she did not want to dance anymore. This act of defiance put her in direct conflict with her mother for the first time. "There were times when I just did not want to do it anymore. And my mother would say, 'You're going!' Mother saw that I had the potential, and she just would not let me quit. She pushed me. But she pushed me nicely."

And her mom's stubbornness served Goldie well a little later on. Through junior high and well into Montgomery Blair High School, dance and song would be Goldie's lone refuge from a social life that was nothing if not dreadful. "I'd stay in my room and play out all the parts in *West Side Story*," she painfully remembered. "Dance made me feel straight and strong. It pulled me up and helped me to outgrow my awkwardness." But all the dance in the world could not totally insulate Hawn from the pain of not being popular, especially with the boys, as she entered her high school years.

"I'd cry a lot and then run home to Mom and ask, 'When am I going to be a wow like the other girls.' Mom always used to reply, 'Don't worry, Goldie. One of these days you won't be able to control all the boys who are going to come around.' And I would say, 'Oh?' and start bawling again."

All her mother's promises could not make a dent in Goldie's low self-esteem, and who could blame her. She would regularly get dolled up for dances and then end up sitting in a corner because nobody would ask her to dance. One particular nightmare remains locked in her mind to this day. "I got all done up, curled my hair, and I went and sat. At one point they played "Misty" by Johnny Mathis, and I sat and watched it all happen. It was so sad."

Goldie's luck went from bad to worse. Her first makeout session with a boy, at age sixteen, was, in her words, "boring and disappointing." She played spin the bottle at a Halloween party in her mid-teens but said, "Every time I'd spin the bottle, it wouldn't point to a soul."

During those years, Goldie tried to curry favor with her peer group by hanging with a tough crowd. Her attempts at rebelling proved mixed. She once participated in a spontaneous bubble-gum-blowing incident in a classroom. To her chagrin, her reputation as a good girl was so entrenched that she was not punished even though others were. She once shoplifted a skirt from a local department store in an attempt to gain respect from the "bad kids." But her mother took the wind out of her sails by laying a guilt trip on her and making her teary-eyed daughter take it back to the store.

Goldie's attempt at being a delinquent did finally result in her getting some much-needed attention from her classmates. Following a night of teen high jinks in and around Takoma Park and a joyride through a graveyard, Goldie was arrested.

"I wanted to be accepted," recalled Hawn of her antisocial acting out. "I wanted to be more assertive and more fun, like the other kids."

But what Goldie lacked in social self-esteem was more than offset by her growing confidence as a singer-dancer and actor. You could see the talent shining through in her performance in the chorus of the high school production of *Carousel* and her showstopping role in *Bye Bye Birdie*. It was a talent not lost on Richard Pioli, her drama teacher and confidant. "She was a natural performer," he said of his prize pupil. "She was real fluid in her dancing and was able to make it look like she was having a great time onstage. She had a real innate talent for performing."

Connie Chung, a future television news anchor of some note, was a year behind Goldie in high school. She also saw the star potential in Hawn. "She was always a star, even when she wasn't doing anything. I remember her being an instructor's assistant in our chemistry class. She would sit up in the front of the room with her unbelievable posture and those spectacular legs. Even at that point in time, she had a great sense of herself."

By this time, largely through her dedication to dance, Hawn had been able to project the mental and emotional toughness necessary to survive her teens and by age seventeen had pretty much put all her social shortcomings aside in favor of the drive to somehow do something with her talents. "I wasn't really aware of whatever talent I had while I was at school." She chuckled years later at the memory of her youthful indecision. "I tended to just discover things as time went on."

Hawn laughingly recalled that her future plans were the subject of much discussion and speculation among her family and friends. "I was the one least likely to succeed anywhere within a twelve-mile radius of our house. I was forgetful, flighty, and sort of light on my feet. There were always discussions in our household about how I'd end up earning a living. So I took typing. But I always figured I'd dance."

While often shy and retiring in social situations, Hawn was a natural-born leader when she stepped out on the dance floor, and so it came as no surprise that Goldie turned her love for dance into a profession when, at the age of seventeen, she opened Goldie's Dancing School.

According to reports from her students, Goldie was everything a teacher should be: kind, patient, and, like her mother, encouraging. And although Hawn, in 1963, enrolled in Washington, D.C.'s American University as a drama major, her heart and soul were leaning toward the teaching life. "I loved what I was doing," Hawn remembered with joy in her voice. "It wasn't like work. My feeling at the time was that if I didn't make it in show business, I'd be quite happy to teach the rest of my life."

College life for Goldie during her freshman year was an eye-opening experience. Her grades were good but not outstanding, and she appeared to enjoy the academic freedom that college life brought her. She developed a larger circle of friends among the more artistically inclined students.

And it was also at seventeen that Goldie found love for the first time. The romance, with a thirty-year-old actor, was swift. Goldie was deeply in love and wanted to get married. But the actor, whom Goldie, to this day, refuses to name, felt that marriage would

17

interfere with his acting career and that rushing into marriage would be something they would both regret. Goldie was heartbroken but knew he was right.

Goldie's frustrations at love fell in line behind her creative frustrations. The possibilities of a real show-business life kept working on her mind. What she knew was that college and the limited opportunities present in Takoma Park would never be a true test of how good she really was. That Goldie was not cut out for the discipline of college life was brought home to her one day when an instructor told her, in the most positive terms, "What are you still doing at university? You should be in Hollywood."

Hawn took her first tentative step in the direction of a career when she began making the rounds of local theater groups in an attempt to hone her acting talents. In 1963 she auditioned for and got her second professional acting role, a bit part in the Williamsburg, Virginia, summer-stock production of *The Common Glory*. Hawn looked back on that experience as "really terrifying but somehow, magical."

When she auditioned for the role of Juliet in the Williamsburg, Virginia, summer-stock production of *Romeo and Juliet* that same year, Goldie turned in a professional, if rough-around-the-edges, reading. "I really wanted that part," reflected Hawn on that audition, "so I memorized the entire part before the audition. The day of the audition, I showed up in belly-button hiphuggers and a midriff top. I don't think the producers were expecting that outfit."

The producers initially balked at the idea of casting the very green and slightly goofy actress in the all-too-serious role. But there was no denying that Hawn brought a certain edginess and urgency to the character of Juliet, which over the years had become rather predictable. With fingers crossed, the producers cast Hawn in Shakespeare's classic tale.

The summer run of *Romeo and Juliet* took place in a 3000-seat amphitheater. Sister Patti recalled one night in particular. "She was incredible as Juliet," she related with no pretense of objectivity. "It started raining right in the middle of the show, but Goldie so mesmerized the audience that nobody left."

Goldie also remembered the night it rained on her parade. "When it started raining, I didn't know what to do. Then I realized that no one had moved."

The local press cited the depth and progressive edge that Goldie had brought to the role. The praise fueled her growing desire to test the real-world waters. The actress finished her successful summer run and was contemplating her return to American University for the fall 1964 semester when she made the decision to leave the halls of academia behind and escape into real life.

Shortly after her eighteenth birthday, Hawn, with a bit of money saved from her teaching jobs, packed her bags and headed for the door. "I'd been training all these years, and I finally decided that I wanted to make use of my dancing skills to try and break into show business," said Goldie of her decision. "I gave myself a deadline of two years to become self-supporting. Either I was going to make it or I'd find something else to do with my life. Because I wasn't about to waste myself on a dream."

Goldie's father had one final word of advice as she prepared to fend for herself for the first time. "Daddy said, 'Don't believe in the world you're going to...because it is not real.'"

3

Cancan...Cry Cry

"I FELT THAT IF I DIDN'T GO TO NEW YORK, THEN I WOULD BE TOO old," said Hawn, still excited at the memory of the day she stood on the Washington, D.C., turnpike, bags at her feet and her thumb out in the classic hitchhiker's pose. "I had a good feeling about the East. I had such trust. Why else would I hitchhike to New York? I just went into that town headfirst."

Hawn's leap into the Big Apple was not without a safety net. Goldie always felt that she was "very practical" and shuddered at the thought of "coming to New York and not having a job or anything." During frequent trips to New York for dance classes during her year at American University, Goldie learned that Bill Black, her instructor, was putting together a show for the 1964 World's Fair. "He asked me if I wanted to be in it, and I said, 'Yeah,' and basically used the promise of a job to justify going to New York."

The promise of a job was all that Hawn had when her ride dropped her off in the heart of New York City. Her excitement knew no bounds as she stared up at the towering skyscrapers. Though people bumped and jostled her as they moved down the sidewalk and Goldie should have been afraid, she was not.

"I was in New York City!" Hawn related with relish. "I didn't even have a place to stay, but I couldn't have been more excited. I was eighteen and in New York, and I loved everything about it."

Hawn checked into the first reasonable hotel she found and began getting the lay of the land. Her first couple of days and nights alone in the big city had the expected effect on Goldie. By day there was a sense of excitement and anxiousness as she walked the streets in search of a permanent address and the first of many purchases of *Daily Variety* and other show-business-casting publications. By night, Goldie became the little girl. She was frightened, intimidated, but determined to make it. A quick study, Goldie, within a week, had moved into a crowded one-bedroom apartment with three other dancers and set about making her way as a dancer.

Hawn's dance instructor made good on his offer of work, and Goldie soon had her first New York job, dancing the cancan as part of a chorus line in the fair's Texas Pavilion. It was not glamorous work. The costume was tacky, the hours were long, and the tourists were more interested in gawking at Goldie's body as she kicked up her legs and making lewd comments than admiring the quality of the dance routine. There was little time to take in the fair and barely enough time for a fast-food lunch. But to Goldie, it was a $180-a-week paycheck, and she was dancing. She was just too happy to complain.

When the World's Fair job ended, Goldie continued living the hand-to-mouth uncertain life of a struggling dancer. She took dance lessons, went out to auditions that did not result in work, and dreamed of her future amid the clutter of her crowded, cockroach-infested apartment. "I'd run out the door and buy *Variety* and study that week's audition notices. It was all a fantasy, of course, because I didn't have the ambition or the courage to go out and audition for the really big class shows. I guess, at that point, I really didn't have a grand plan."

Nor did Hawn have a lot in the way of street smarts when it came to dealing with the predators that inhabited much of New York's dance world. She would blindly audition, not thinking that the producers and casting agents might be more interested in giving her a one-way ticket to the casting couch.

"A lot of the dance auditions I went to were really awful," Goldie recalled with disgust in her voice. "I went to auditions where all the casting people wanted to do was fuck me. You would see guys literally hanging around for no other purpose than to try and pick up women. There were men in elevators, people in subways...feeling me up and hurting me."

"I had only been in New York a couple of months," Hawn said with a sigh, "and I was not very savvy. I really thought I was in those offices for honest reasons. I didn't have a clue when I was confronted with those kinds of situations."

But what Hawn did have was an aura of innocent sexuality. It was something she projected to the world without even thinking about it. And it made her an immediate target of the more unscrupulous elements of her profession.

Consequently, when Goldie was approached one day on Manhattan's Upper West Side by a man claiming to be the representative for a famous cartoonist and promising "she would get a big part in an upcoming show if she were nice to him," Goldie fell for it hook, line, and sinker.

It all appeared legit. He had given her some lines to rehearse and told her to come to his apartment at an appointed time. Goldie's dancer-roommates warned her that the proposal smelled like trouble. Goldie saw nothing wrong until she went to the apartment and walked through the door.

Goldie remembered the scene. "The cartoonist was there, and he was dressed in this dressing gown. He asked me to turn around, show him my legs, and put some beads in my mouth. Then he asked me to sit down on the couch next to him." The cartoonist opened his robe and exposed himself. Goldie's eyes grew wide in horror. The real reason she was there was immediately evident. She got furious, then hysterical.

"I guess I reacted the way any eighteen-year-old would. He told me that he would take me to Hollywood and that I would be a big star, but when I wouldn't go for it, he got real nasty. He said, 'Go back home and marry a Jewish dentist, because you'll never get anywhere.' I was real angry at that point. I said, 'Well, if that's what I'm going to have to do, then I will, and I ran out. It was a frightening experience. But I felt I knew the difference between right and wrong."

Goldie's sense of right and wrong short-circuited one of her next jobs, dancing as part of a touring rock-and-roll band's stage show. For Goldie, her first touring experience was an eye-opener. She reveled in the panorama of places and people that flashed before her eyes. The venues the band played in were rarely top of the line, but Goldie was gathering a boatload of new experiences that she knew would linger in her memory.

Everything was fine until the band got to Puerto Rico and Goldie discovered that the dancers were making a lot less than the musicians. She was not experienced enough to realize that, unfortunately, this was common practice. All she knew was that it was unfair. So she complained, demanded more money, and was promptly fired.

Hawn returned to the States with two hundred dollars severance pay. The money could have been better spent paying the rent, but Goldie, in one of her many impulsive moves, went out and bought a dog instead. Goldie sighed at the memory of that purchase. "I guess I just needed a friend."

Back in New York, Hawn continued to scan the casting notices and audition for everything in sight. She tried out to be a dancer at the famed Copacabana nightclub but did not get a callback. Broadway opportunities at the time were few and far between, and while she would occasionally go for the upscale auditions, she was not surprised when the fierce competition resulted in her striking out. Off-Broadway auditions were equally fierce and consequently just as unrewarding.

With even scarce, mid-level jobs hard to find and with money either tight or nonexistent, Hawn resorted to the then thriving and often sleazy go-go dancer trade in bars and strip clubs up and down the East Coast. "I had to make a buck, you know?" Hawn once said defensively of her decision to dance in cages and on tabletops in front of rowdy, disgusting drunks. "So I hooked up with this go-go dancing agent on Sixth Avenue and would go down there when things got tight and say, 'Do you have anything for me today?'"

What the agent would often have for Goldie was jobs in joints like New York's then notorious Dudes 'n' Dolls and other seedy places where Hawn would dance, sometimes in pasties but never topless, in front of leering drunks for as little as ten dollars a night. Goldie recalled that go-go dancing became an endless parade of horrors but cites one gig in particular, at the Peppermint Box, in New Jersey, as an example of how bad it could get.

She barely had the bus fare, and as the miles in New Jersey flew by, Hawn stared out the bus window with a bad feeling about the job. Was it worth the twenty-five dollars she had been promised? Her worst fears were confirmed when she walked through the Peppermint Box's front door. "It was the worst bar you could possibly imagine," she painfully recalled. "It was dark, sleazy, and dirty."

The lone barmaid pointed Hawn in the direction of the bar owner, who, even at this early hour, was drunk. He immediately began to put the moves, as well as his hands, on Goldie. She rejected his advances and, trying to be all business, wanted to know where she would be dancing. He pointed to a wobbly, three-legged table in front of four drunk customers, who, having spotted Hawn, began to chant, 'Make her dance! Make her dance!'

Goldie's instincts told her she should run right out the door. But the reality was that she did not have enough money for bus fare back to the city. So she stepped up on the table and began doing a halfhearted go-go dance as Dean Martin's *Everybody Loves Somebody Sometime* blared out of cheap speakers.

"There was this man sitting at the bar looking at me, and I thought he was being sympathetic," said Hawn, describing the dance before "that den of perverts. Well he wasn't. At one point, I turned around and he had pulled out his cock and was jerking off. I freaked and began dancing faster and faster. Finally, my knees buckled, and I thought I was going to faint. I climbed off the table and went to find the boss. He had passed out, so I couldn't get my money, and since the buses had stopped running, I was stuck in Jersey in the middle of the night with no way home."

Desperation made her willing to take a gamble, and she looked around the bar at the patrons. "There were four men sitting at the bar. I went up to the two men I thought looked the nicest and asked them if they would drive me home. They were truck drivers. So I ended up riding back to New York that night in a Mack truck."

Goldie could not be blamed for feeling extremely suspicious of the opposite sex in the face of these seemingly endless assaults on her character and soul. As always, however, she remained positive. "I really liked men," Goldie said, looking back on those go-go days. "And it always amazed me that I could continue to like them."

Hawn's luck continued to be bad in other than business dealings. Goldie and some friends were driving on the West Side Highway in 1965 when their car was involved in an auto accident. She was knocked unconscious and taken to a nearby hospital, where she eventually came to about an hour later. Her attending physician said that she was lucky to be alive. Though she suffered only minor physical injuries, the accident did take its toll on Hawn emotionally.

"After the accident I went through a period of severe anxiety. For a long time I couldn't ride in a car that I wasn't driving."

Despite continuing to face a seemingly endless series of dance jobs, Hawn refused to take a less threatening dues-paying job as a waitress.

"I was a dancer, and that's what I did. I had to keep my body working even if it was in unpleasant situations. As a dancer, I was getting to see the world from the bottom. We got the shit kicked out of us, and we saw all kinds of questionable behavior. But the bad experiences were not necessarily totally bad. I learned from working at the bottom and looking around at the dregs of society."

During these tough times, Goldie could always count on a kind word and some money from her parents, who were painfully aware of what their daughter was going through. Although they knew it would fall on deaf ears, Edward and Laura would regularly tell their daughter that she could come home anytime she wanted and that there would be no shame in doing so.

"I would get very upset when Goldie would tell me what was happening to her in New York," said Laura Hawn. "I was sending her money for her dance lessons and expenses so she would not have to do those awful things. But she kept saying it was something she had to do."

25

Her father was more to the point. "He said I could always come home."

Eventually, Hawn downsized her living conditions, moving into an Eighth Avenue apartment complex (in the rough part of town called Hell's Kitchen) that had the requisite roaches and the added attraction of hookers and junkies in the halls and outside the building. Goldie, while occasionally fending off muggers and watching more than one drug deal go down, put the best possible face on her situation, claiming that it was just something she had to do to stay in New York and be in show business.

Goldie persisted. But by 1966 she began to get ground down by the seemingly endless hustle and the fact that she was going nowhere in her career. Hawn was seriously thinking of packing it in and going back to Takoma Park when she received a telephone call from a choreographer with the offer to work in some West Coast tent musicals. The choreographer enthusiastically extolled the virtues of California as a happening place and predicted that something big would happen for her in Los Angeles.

Hawn, burned out on New York and a big believer in intuition, did not need much convincing. She packed her belongings and her dog into her car, and after saying goodbye to her handful of friends, she left New York for the West Coast. Goldie was hopeful as she watched the landscape race by and change from smooth to undulating to mountainous on the journey to Los Angeles. After a year and a half of New York disappointments, Hawn had no illusions when she finally set foot in the City of Angels. She would be leery of come-ons, suspicious of offers that were too good to be true, and determined to be as straightforward as possible in her approach to breaking into show business. "I was just trying to find a way to make a living as a professional dancer," said Hawn, the first signs of cynicism beginning to creep into her mind-set.

True to his promise, the choreographer hooked the young dancer up with a chorus job in a production of *Pal Joey* at the famed Anaheim, California, Melodyland Theater. While light-years up the scale from go-go dancing, *Pal Joey* and the productions that followed it were all conspicuous by their long hours and low pay. But Goldie didn't care; in her heart of hearts she knew that this was a step in the right direction.

Goldie would call home with good and bad news and would take comfort in the wisdom and advice her parents would offer. It was during those calls home that Goldie discovered that no subject was taboo. "When I first got to California, I was having a terrible, stupid love affair with this guy who didn't care for me at all. Well, my daddy sent me a letter that said, 'Don't ever feel you're alone. There's no way to get away from the love your mother and I feel for you.' That letter pulled me through."

It was during this dues-paying period that Goldie met and immediately fell in love with a choreographer-actor named Gus Trikonis.

"Goldie was so full of life," Trikonis said years later of his first impression of Hawn. "She was so quick and so clever. For me, Goldie was amusement at first sight. There was something quite vulnerable about Goldie that immediately made me want to watch out for her."

Gus Trikonis was cut from classic Greek stock. He had dark good looks, passion, and an electric intensity. He could joke with the best of them. But once rehearsals started, he was strictly business. Those qualities, recalled Goldie, were not what sealed their love at first sight. "He was so sensitive. So marvelously sensitive. And he was so totally honest and understanding." Given Goldie's lighthearted, impulsive qualities, the couple appeared to be the perfect match.

Their love flourished during the run at Melodyland. When they were not in intense rehearsals and performing an endless run of shows, Trikonis and Hawn were inseparable. It was rare when they were not found hugging and hand-holding. "Gus and I were the same age, and we were both Scorpios. We had fun together. It was a good time."

Trikonis saw those heady first days with Goldie as something truly special. "Those were marvelous days. We were flat broke, but we were never lonely. Friends dropped by all the time, and most of all, we had each other. We shared everything. That's what made our relationship so special."

But while Hawn's romantic life had taken a turn for the better, professionally she was still treading water. After Melodyland's season ended, she discovered that jobs for dancers were difficult to come by. While she did manage to land parts in touring productions of *Kiss Me Kate* and *Guys and Dolls* that offered more experience and a steady paycheck for a while, she knew that when those jobs eventually ended, she would be reduced to go-go dancing jobs or even worse if she stayed in Los Angeles. Trikonis could be of little help, for he was in the same boat. It also did not help their collective feelings of loneliness when, at about the time Hawn returned from the road, Trikonis was occupied with jobs in productions of *Bajour* and *West Side Story*.

Consequently, when it came to Trikonis, Goldie was feeling insecure, part of which stemmed from her uncertainty about experiencing real love for the first time and what dealing with those emotions entailed. But she did recall feelings of jealousy during this period and visited a psychic on a whim. The psychic, after going through the usual mumbo jumbo, happily proclaimed to Hawn: "You have stardom written all over your forehead." Goldie's response was immediate. "Yeah. Sure. Is my boyfriend fucking somebody or not?"

Fate intervened in the form of an offer for Hawn to dance in the chorus line at the Desert Inn Hotel in Las Vegas. It was dancing, and it was a regular paycheck, and so, after a tearful departure from Trikonis during which they promised to call and visit each other regularly, she once again packed her belongings and, with her dog, headed out into the desert.

Goldie, given her history of dancing in less than ideal situations, was not surprised at what greeted her at the Desert Inn. Her hours were a hellish ten at night until five in the morning. She was dancing in four hour-and-a-half shows a night. It was rough, and it was taking its toll.

"You had to move at a fever pitch," remembered Hawn of those nights on the Vegas stage, high-stepping in front of often uninterested and intoxicated audiences. "If you weren't moving at a fever pitch, you would be fired. I was a zombie. I realized that I was temperamentally and morally unsuited for the nightclub work that I was doing, and yet there I was, doing it, anyway. It was the saddest time of my life."

While in Vegas, Goldie landed a part in a commercial for a brand of hair spray. She savored this first appearance in front of the camera, so much so that she barely protested when someone covered up her blond hair with a fire-engine-red wig. Her delight was short-lived. "I wasn't thrilled when I finally saw the commercial," reflected Hawn. "I was playing your basic dumb blonde in a red wig."

One morning, after yet another punishing night at the Desert Inn and only an hour after falling into a fitful sleep, she woke up with a start—and a trademark impulsive revelation. "I just had this hunch that I would do better in Los Angeles. So I packed up all my belongings and the dog, put them in the car, and left immediately for Los Angeles. I knew Hollywood could not be much worse."

Hawn did not realize it at the time, but emotionally she was in a very fragile state. The cross-country odyssey, the lack of success, the lousy jobs, and, finally, the fact that she was alone much of the time were beginning to weigh on her.

Goldie's self-imposed goals upon arriving in Los Angeles for the second time were indicative of a mind racing potentially, and dangerously, out of control. She proclaimed that if she did not make it big in two weeks, she was going back to Takoma Park. Hawn then modified that deadline, giving herself nine months to make it before saying she would go on the road as part of a song-and-dance act.

It was a good thing she did, because the Los Angeles she had left was still the same when she returned, and auditions turned into rejections or the usual come-ons.

"There was this one producer who wanted to give me a job," the actress recalled with a sad sense of irony in later years. "He said I'd probably make lots of money and probably be a star if I'd just...put across (sexually). I told him, 'I would never take a job that way.' And he said, 'Then you'll never get anywhere in this business.' I told him, 'I don't care.' And I really didn't care, because at that time I was more interested in making a living as a professional dancer than I was in being a celebrity. But I have to admit that the idea of that proposition really hurt."

29

Hawn persisted. She auditioned for everything and anything and got nothing. The constant blows to her ego and her already fragile emotional state had put her, she painfully remembered, within shouting distance of a nervous breakdown. "I was a mess. I was upset. I was wondering what mattered. And I was struggling for an answer."

Goldie turned twenty-one in 1966. Her relationship with Gus Trikonis continued to be the lone bright spot. But given the nomadic nature of being a dancer, they would often find themselves apart, which played into Hawn's insecurities. "I was always jealous of Gus when I first met him. I was apprehensive about other women being around him."

It appeared that Goldie was going to have to face her own deadline of nine months with failure. Mentally she was preparing for a song-and-dance life on the road. Suddenly her luck changed.

Andy Griffith, who was coming to the end of a highly successful run as the good-natured sheriff of Mayberry on *The Andy Griffith Show,* was spreading his wings with a singing-dancing-comedy special. Dancing was the operative word for Hawn, who, operating on instinct rather than drive and enthusiasm at this point, auditioned for the special.

She arrived for the audition in an upbeat mood. There was no mistaking that wide-eyed enthusiasm as anything other than real. Goldie had dug down deep inside and had rediscovered what she liked about dancing, which was everything. Griffith and the show's producers were dazzled by her agility, style, and the personality she projected while executing complex dance movements. She was hired on the spot.

William Morris agent Art Simon was a practiced hand at spotting new talent, and so he made a historic snap judgment while watching the taping of the Andy Griffith special in early 1967. He decided that Goldie Hawn had something extra. "That girl certainly had something special," recalled Simon of the night he first saw Hawn. "You could see that she was not the stereotypical chorus girl."

After the program was taped, Simon went backstage, introduced himself to Hawn, and gave her his card. "I asked her if she did anything besides dance, and she thought I was propositioning her. So she refused to call me. Finally, I called and explained everything to her, and she signed on with William Morris."

With a high-powered agency in her corner, it was not long before Hawn was going out on auditions that were higher profile than what she was used to. One of the first was for a fall 1967 television situation comedy called *Good Morning World*.

The show, developed by *The Dick Van Dyke Show* creative team of Carl Reiner, Sheldon Leonard, Bill Persky, and Sam Denoff, focused on the comic possibilities of two Los Angeles radio disc jockeys and their high jinks on and off the air. Hawn was sent in to read for the role of the wife of one of the DJs. Rather than simply reading her lines, Hawn brought along a prop. The image of her reading her lines while holding a teapot struck a chord with the show's producers, and Hawn walked out with a part. But, recalled show producer Sam Persky, it was not the part she was up for.

"Goldie auditioned for the wife of one of the DJs but didn't get it. But we were so impressed with her that we told her that we had another part for her. She said, 'What is it?' We said we don't know because we haven't written that part into the show yet. But we told her that she would definitely be in the show." That part ultimately turned out to be the character of Sandy, a dingbat next-door neighbor who has a crush on one of the DJs.

Hawn, in those heady early days of *Good Morning World*, was experiencing both the upside and the downside of celebrity firsthand. Overnight she had gone from a nobody with simple values and a low-key life to a performer who was now recognized by millions and was having to deal with the trappings of stardom. "Suddenly I was starring in this series, and people were asking me for my autograph. My life was changing so fast."

In the meantime, Trikonis was battling his own demons—the insecurity and confusion common to most entertainers—and had entered therapy. Preaching the line of the converted, he regaled Hawn with how far he had come in analysis and eventually persuaded her to also get counseling.

Unlike Trikonis, Hawn stopped short of jumping completely

into the therapy process. At first, she thought she could handle her emotions and could overcome the conflict between the traditional little girl and the fantasy of Hollywood that was becoming her life. But she finally caved in during one emotional session and confided to her therapist, "I want to be normal. I just want to be normal."

On paper *Good Morning World* appeared to have some potential. When the show aired for the first time on ABC on September 5, 1967, everybody knew how unfunny a comedy show could be.

Good Morning World was perceived as a bomb from the word go. The scripts were contrived; the stories were hackneyed; the laughs were forced. Only Hawn, who was regularly handed such allegedly funny lines as "I have to go home and get my roast out of the clothes dryer," stood out in this uncomedic mishmash. But critical barbs aside, Hawn found the experience fresh and exciting.

"I was playing your typical girl-next-door part. And just about everything that was happening on the show was a new experience for me. I had never had anybody put a clapboard in front of my face and say, "Take one," before. The first time it happened, my voice suddenly went up eight octaves, and everybody laughed."

When not shooting *Good Morning World,* Hawn was a constant bubbly presence on the Paramount Studios lot where the show was being filmed. Up-and-coming director Garry Marshall would regularly run into Goldie at the studio commissary or wandering down streets and alleys between soundstages. He recalled his perception of Goldie as just another chorus girl on the loose. "She was kind of this kooky girl who seemed to be running around," Marshall reported. "She was a dancer who was going to act. At that point, I wasn't taking her too seriously."

Not content to let Goldie rest on her days off, the folks at William Morris were constantly sending her out on auditions. It was on one of these outside jaunts that Goldie landed a very small role as a dancer in Disney's sickeningly sweet film *The One and Only Genuine Original Family Band* (1968), a thin, saccharine tale of a musical family's falling-out over a presidential election. The actress, looking back on her first film role, laughingly said it was not a real meaty part. "I was the lead dancer. They called me the giggly girl."

Hawn did have memories of the young actor who played one of the children's roles, Kurt Russell. "I remember Kurt very well," she recalled slyly in later years. "I remember he was five years younger than me and that he always seemed to be watching me when I was limbering up. But we didn't say much of anything to each other except hello."

Russell also had memories of that first meeting. "I remember thinking that she was real well built. But I was [a kid] and I didn't have a car or anything, so I felt she was just beyond the realm of possibility for me."

Television executives were a more patient lot back then, and so *Good Morning World* was allowed to run out its protracted thirteen-episode course before the plug was mercifully pulled (after a number of reruns) after the final episode aired on September 15, 1968. But by Christmas 1967, when the show had already been given its pink slip, producer George Schlatter, who was putting together an idea for a free-form comedy-sketch show, called up Goldie's agent to inquire as to whether she was available for the new project that was to be called *Laugh-In*.

"He thought I was funny in some way that he couldn't explain," Hawn said, giggling. "He didn't have any idea what I could do."

4

Dumb...Like a Fox

ROWAN AND MARTIN'S LAUGH-IN WAS A BIG GAMBLE IN 1968.

The times had definitely changed in the wake of an unpopular war in Vietnam, the peace and love movement and the specter of Richard Nixon, looming on the horizon. For most of the world, these events were serious business. For producer George Schlatter, folks seemed ripe for a laugh—rather, a thousand laughs. Thus was born *Rowan and Martin's Laugh-In*, a maddening, seemingly unstructured nonstop run of comedy sketches, one-liners, zany characters, and all manner of satire aimed at the popular and unpopular cultural targets of the day.

How much of a risk was *Laugh-In*? Even with Schlatter's long-standing reputation and the star power of the show's hosts, the comedy team of Dan Rowan and Dick Martin, the NBC executives were offering no guarantees. They knew they had a tiger by the tail. So did Schlatter.

Schlatter could not put his finger on why he hired Goldie Hawn. "We hired her because she could dance and because she looked kind of cute," the producer said of his cockeyed reasoning. "So, initially, we hired her to be one of the dozen girls who would dance in the background on the show."

Goldie was aware of the uncertainty as she prepared for the

audition. More established performers like Gary Owens and Ruth Buzzi and hyped newcomers like Theresa Graves, were being offered a minimum one-season contract. If she made the cut, Goldie's deal would be for only three shows.

Dan Rowan remembered Hawn's first visit to the production office as a truly magic moment. "She walked in and said hello. George and Dick and I just looked at each other and said, 'She's in.'"

Cohost Dick Martin agreed with Schlatter and Rowan's first impressions. "When she first came in to read, she was charming. She had this giggle that was just so delightful."

Given the vagaries of Schlatter's reasons for hiring her, it was no surprise that Goldie was like a babe in the woods the day she arrived for formal screen tests and auditions at the NBC studios. Hawn had seen a lot of strange things in her fledgling career, but nothing had prepared her for the circus troupe that were her costars. Seasoned pros like Gary Owens and Ruth Buzzi were laughing and doing shtick. Newcomers like Judy Carne and Theresa Graves were all smiles, laughs, and jokes. All had distinctive personalities, and all seemed to be coming at Goldie at once. Goldie was cautious at first, feeling a bit overwhelmed, but she eventually warmed to them and would in time become fast friends with many of them. But first she had to prove to the producers that she belonged.

"Nobody seemed to have a clue as to what I could do," she recalled of the day she met Rowan and Martin and the rest of the *Laugh-In* cast. "I never considered myself funny, and I'd hardly ever acted before. So I just stood there, waiting for somebody to tell me what to do."

And so the great *Laugh-In* experiment began, with Schlatter tinkering with Goldie's character like Frankenstein with his monster. Initially, Hawn was tested in a straight role, reading reports for a skit called "The News of the Future." But an admittedly confused and nervous Goldie read the wrong cue cards and promptly erupted into uncontrollable giggles.

There was something infectious in Goldie's response, and the assembled cast and crew likewise broke into gales of laughter. Everybody calmed down, and Goldie tried the straight reading again. Once again she misread the cards. Once again she started giggling.

"I just got scared, read the wrong cards, and started giggling. I was nervous, and that was my reaction. I was scared to death, and I couldn't understand why everybody was laughing. It didn't seem all that funny to me."

A lightbulb went on in George Schlatter's head. He had found Goldie Hawn's character—the nervous, scared, innocent child who could brush away the fears with a laugh. "At that moment, I saw her as an original," the producer reflected. "She was the woman-child; sweet, vulnerable, sexy, and fun."

While Goldie stood perplexed and flustered, Schlatter tested his theory one more time to make sure what they had stumbled upon was real. "We started switching the cue cards on purpose. And again we had the giggles. It was perfect."

Once she recovered her composure, Goldie was able to see the method in Schlatter's madness. She still did not see herself as funny. "It just turned out that being confused was my thing and that character was born at that moment."

But Schlatter knew that confusion alone would not stand the test of time, and so the *Laugh-In* writers, taking their cue from Goldie, began fleshing out her character. It was not uncommon during those rehearsals for the writers to assemble on the *Laugh-In* set ostensibly to watch the entire cast but with all eyes on Goldie, watching for a move, a look, or a speech pattern that would help them find her niche.

A lot came from those sessions. Fractured, nonsensical sentences, such as "A chrysanthemum by any other name would be easier to pronounce,'" and "What do I care? I'm Polish," quickly became a part of her laugh bag. So did mistiming, taking that extra beat or two that would throw off her response to a joke or question. As part of the ongoing party set piece and blackout bits, Goldie would often be clad in a bikini, and painted head to toe with witty sayings or symbols. By the time Rowan and Martin's *Laugh-In* filmed its first episode late in 1967, the package was complete.

When the show debuted to much fanfare on January 22, 1968,

Goldie Hawn's character was still very much a work in progress that everybody connected to the show took great relish in contributing to. A spontaneous exchange between Hawn and Schlatter during the taping of one show resulted in the catchphrase "poor baby" being added to her repertoire of giggle-inducing moments that included the entire cast's classic "Sock it to me." Eliciting Goldie's giggle in new and novel ways became a personal challenge to the cue-card people. Cards would inevitably wind up mixed up, upside down, or backward. Sometimes the cards would contain dirty words or sometimes just a picture. The result was always the same: Goldie would burst into unforced laughter.

The rest is television history. An estimated 50 million people tuned in to that first show and became loyal fans. Hawn was immediately rewarded with a long-term contract. Her frugging, body-painted innocent became the centerpiece of the show. The media, quick to blur the line between reality and fantasy, wasted little time in jumping on Goldie's *Laugh-In* persona and posed the question of how dumb or smart Goldie Hawn actually was. Those connected to the show leaped to Goldie's defense.

"Yeah, Goldie's dumb," said Dick Martin chuckling. "Dumb like a fox."

Schlatter, always available to add laughter to any mix, told a reporter during the heyday of *Laugh-In,* "She's not dumb. Her head just wanders a little, that's all."

How smart Goldie actually was became only one of the questions the actress had to field during that first season. Her TV image, in the eyes of the growing feminist movement, was running contrary to the notion of self-determination and empowerment of women. She laughed at the idea that she was a dumb go-go dancer playing into men's fantasies of the ideal woman. "That's just a role. I always knew that I was smart, and I felt I was already liberated, so what they were asking just didn't seem to make sense."

The first season of *Laugh-In* was a revelation for Goldie on a number of fronts, the most taxing being her reality versus the fantasy of Hollywood. Her middle-class, Maryland upbringing had not prepared her for the onslaught of Hollywood hype that *Laugh-*

In's success was forcing her to deal with. She was hesitant in the face of the star-making process that she had long sought, albeit on a more comfortable, fantasy level.

"It was a whole different world," offered Hawn in reflecting on those crazy days. "I wasn't doing what I was trained to do. My position in life was changing, and my friends and their jobs were all shifting. I didn't know where I was going."

Goldie recalled those days as a confusing time, with "no walls and no perimeters." She admitted to being frightened and in need of security. At the same time, she was wide-eyed at the universe that was unfolding before her.

"I was twenty-two years old. I was just happy to have a job. But I really didn't have any idea what was happening. I was this new fresh face on the scene, and everybody embraced me. I was sort of an inkblot. People would see what they wanted or needed to see, and that didn't have much to do with who I really was. But at that point what was going on was more about hype and not about my talent. The reality was that I was already typecast."

Schlatter disagreed. In his mind the talent was definitely there. "Directing Goldie was more a matter of getting out of the way, because whatever was going to happen was better than what I would have directed her to do. She was obviously superbright and had a very good sense of physical comedy."

Carol Channing, who worked with Hawn as a guest star in the early days of *Laugh-In*, agreed with Schlatter. "I knew immediately I was working with another George Burns."

The long hours spent turning out a *Laugh-In* hour required a lot of patience. The challenge lay in creating scenes that on-screen had to appear as spontaneous but which, in reality, might require ten or more takes to get right.

"To keep something like what we were doing on *Laugh-In* as fresh, easy, and spontaneous as it seemed was probably one of the most difficult and disciplining things I had ever done," Goldie recalled of *Laugh-In*'s grueling schedule. "It's easy to bring tears, but to bring laughter is very difficult. The timing took hard work, concentration, and a great deal of practice."

Hawn took solace in the fact that after the sixteen hours it took to film one episode of *Laugh-In*, she could retreat into some semblance of normalcy. "I would look forward to coming home from NBC, making dinner, and being with Gus."

And Trikonis, to his credit, was there for her. He could be counted on to lend an ear or a shoulder as Goldie unloaded the events of the day. When she was too tired to cook dinner, he would throw something together or insist they go out for a bite at some out-of-the-way cafe. Goldie could not love Gus more if she tried.

But it was to be expected that the level of Goldie's success would eventually begin to affect her relationship with Trikonis. The choreographer had made a career correction and was attempting to make it in Hollywood as a director, with no results. While Trikonis was struggling, Goldie was making the headlines and, ultimately even more detrimental to the relationship, all the money.

"I felt I should be the breadwinner," said a candid Trikonis years later. "Her success became an incredible threat to my ego."

"He's Greek," Hawn said of those bumps in their relationship. "It's very important for Greek men to bring home the bread and butter. And it was tough because, while everything was happening for me, nothing was happening for him."

Hawn was aware of the friction in the relationship and did her best to include Trikonis in whatever was going on in her universe. She would talk him up in interviews, and he was always on her arm when she attended Hollywood parties. Goldie would get excited at even a tiny blip on Trikonis's career horizon. Goldie was hoping fervently that his success would come to equal hers.

Nevertheless, Goldie's career continued to occupy her thoughts. By mid-season, the popularity of *Laugh-In* had cemented her celebrity, and Goldie was beginning to feel its downside. She could not walk down the street without strangers coming up to her and asking her to giggle. Sometimes she would do it. But just as often she was beginning to say no. Her anxiety level was high. She could not go into a restaurant without getting nauseous and sometimes throwing up. She finally stopped going out altogether. Her world had become the path between her home and the *Laugh-In* studio.

"The big-star stuff came when I hit *Laugh-In*," she reflected. "I was in everybody's living room. When I'd walk out on the street, everybody thought they knew me."

Her adverse reaction to stardom was not lost on her mother. She would call her regularly, and during those conversations she was once again the little girl. "It was the toughest period of my daughter's life," Laura Hawn reported. "She couldn't come to terms with the world of success. Goldie always needed a nest and security. The sudden stardom offered her nothing to hold on to. She would call me crying, saying, 'I don't want to be a star.'"

During her visits, Laura Hawn would often attempt to shield her daughter from the onslaught of celebrity. She and Goldie were eating breakfast in a Los Angeles restaurant one day when a woman approached their table and began to babble about how wonderful Goldie was. Goldie was polite, but as the woman continued to hover and talk, Laura began to get upset. Finally, she snapped. "Would you kindly let her eat her breakfast!" Laura recalled with a laugh. "Goldie got this horrified look on her face and said, 'Mother! How could you do that?' And I said, 'Very easily.'"

Goldie was having a love-hate relationship with her star status. On one level she craved it. But she was equally candid in explaining the price she was paying. "I began having anxiety attacks when I started becoming successful. They kept coming, and I couldn't understand them. I'd get dizzy when I went out in public."

Hawn reasoned that a big part of her problem centered on the fact that her *Laugh-In* persona had become bigger than life and the real Goldie was losing her identity in the process. "I was afraid the me, the little Goldie, would get lost," she admitted. "I was frustrated at times that the very thing that was making me a star was also locking me in. I was afraid that I would change or that I would be consumed by the business. I definitely felt split as a personality. On *Laugh-In*, I was carefree and zany. Off camera, I was a wreck. I had trouble coping with day-to-day living."

Goldie's downward spiral manifested itself in her seeking total solitude. When not at the studio, she would hide out in her home, sip tea, and watch television. The physical workout on *Laugh-In*, coupled with the fact that she was now eating very little, resulted in a drastic weight loss. At her lowest point, the five-foot-six actress weighed a mere ninety-six pounds.

Goldie was slow to come around; she felt that the stresses in her life were something she could handle. But she finally admitted that she needed help and consented to full-blown therapy. She recalled years later that those early sessions were a frightening experience in which she addressed "the dichotomy" of the real Goldie and the television Goldie. "In the beginning of my analysis, I was afraid I was losing myself. The real reason that I got professional help was that I felt I was beginning to lose my joy. What I began to eventually get out of therapy was clarity. I saw that I was never really my image and that I was basically a very serious person."

Laura Hawn was admittedly skeptical about Hawn's analysis, especially when her daughter expressed doubts to her about her dancing at an early age. "But her years of analysis strengthened her more than anyone could imagine. I knew she was gaining a lot from it."

So did Goldie. She was becoming stronger and more self-confident. The wacky Goldie of *Laugh-In* was a constant with which she was slowly but surely coming to terms. The real Goldie, she was certain, would survive in both her personal and professional life. Hawn, who turned twenty-three during the hiatus on *Laugh-In*, also found that therapy had also enhanced her love for Trikonis, pointing to him as a calming presence and a quietly passionate counter to her own personality. "I fell in love [with Gus] because he is the strong, determined man he is," she cooed. "I never wanted to marry a weakling."

Yes, marriage was very much on her mind. In fact, Hawn took regular comfort from the craziness of Hollywood in fantasies of marriage, children, and a white-picket-fence life. "I want to be married," she reported early in 1969. "I want an honest relationship with a man. I don't want to be some kind of half-baked floozy who lives with whichever man interests her for the present and then moves on to another."

Goldie Hawn and Gus Trikonis were married in Honolulu in

1969. Despite her celebrity status, they were able to pull off their nuptials, performed by a local justice of the peace, in total secrecy. Serving as the surrogate father of the bride in this spur-of-the-moment ceremony was Hawn's agent, Art Simon. In typical Goldie fashion, the groom wore blue jeans and the bride wore green silk hiphuggers and a massive gardenia on her head. Goldie beamed following the ceremony that officially made Gus and Goldie husband and wife. "When I started out, what I wanted most was to marry the husband I wanted and to have the house I wanted. Now I have both."

What they did not have was much time for a honeymoon. Art Simon had been working overtime to capitalize on Hawn's high television profile. Consequently, Goldie barely had time to get used to the idea of being Goldie Trikonis when she was offered her first substantial film role.

Cactus Flower, based on the original Broadway play, told the heartwarming story of a successful dentist's plain-Jane nurse who blossoms into a loving woman when she discovers she's in love with her boss. With Ingrid Bergman and Walter Matthau already onboard in the lead roles, *Cactus Flower* was a high-profile project. Goldie was being courted for the role of Toni, the dentist's kookie girlfriend. It was the kind of role most actresses would jump at.

Goldie said thanks but no thanks.

Studio executive Billy Wilder had taken a shine to Goldie and wanted her to come in and test for the role. Goldie, with more than a little guidance from Simon, decided that producers had seen enough of her work, and while she was definitely available, she felt she was above the formality of an audition. Hawn's decision seemed the height of insanity. She had nothing to gain and everything to lose by appearing difficult this early in her career. It was a calculated risk because Goldie, anxious to take the next step toward a full-time film career, wanted the part, but on her terms.

The actress reflected on the reason for her no-audition edict: "I felt like I really understood the character of Toni. I felt, through some of the experiences I had, I was a bit like this character."

Days went by while *Cactus Flower's* producer Mike Frankovich and director Gene Saks pondered the risks inherent in casting a television star in a pivotal role in a big-budget motion picture. Ultimately, they wanted her enough to take the chance and sign her. Goldie readily agreed to a $50,000 payday. Frankovich, with his practiced eye for talent, felt that Hawn was a bargain at twice the price and, as an afterthought, insisted that the actress sign a four-picture deal with Columbia Pictures. Goldie was a bit hesitant, but Simon, who liked the idea of his client's constantly working, recommended that she go for it. Goldie signed the four-picture deal.

Goldie felt she had made the right decision, but her mother expressed some doubts about how Goldie's jumping in to movies would affect her status on *Laugh-In*. "She said she wanted to grow," Laura Hawn said. "So she took the part in *Cactus Flower* to prove that she could grow. I was fearful, but I knew from experience that Goldie always made the right decisions."

Goldie knew she was taking a chance by agreeing to such a high-profile film so early in her career. "I'm not a skilled actress," she said at the time. "But I've had some experience. It's useless for me to take acting lessons at this point. Now I think it's just a matter of experience and timing."

Hawn's talking up of Trikonis's talents caught the interest of the *Cactus Flower* producers, who hired him to direct the making of a promotional feature for the film. On the surface it appeared to be little more than a mercy job created to keep the star happy. Goldie was not thinking so much in terms of getting her husband a job. All she knew was that Gus and she would not have to be apart.

Goldie reported to the set of *Cactus Flower* in midsummer 1969 amid press speculations that she, a mere babe in the woods, would be eaten alive by the legendary talents of Bergman and Matthau. Goldie was warned that the often volatile Matthau could be less than charitable to other actors. Goldie, however, did not heed the warnings and concerned herself with the I. A. L. Diamond script, which she felt represented an ideal opportunity to stretch as an actress.

"*Cactus Flower* gave me a chance to prove that I had a heavy side," she proclaimed. "The character of Toni had more depth and color than anything I had ever done before."

Hawn took *Cactus Flower* very seriously. She was on time. She knew her lines. Director Saks was amazed by the professionalism he found in what he perceived to be another ditzy blond actress. "I knew it was her first film, so I was probably expecting the worst. But I can honestly say that I've never had a girl in her first film be so professional."

Goldie did have some moments of panic during the first few days of filming. "I was so intimidated that I thought I would not be able to function." But after she got over her insecurities, Goldie's bubbly personality and innocence alternately amused and charmed Bergman and Matthau. The actors were quick to cite Hawn's talent and professionalism. Matthau was particularly enthralled with Hawn. "She warms your insides like a bowl of porridge," he quipped. "She has talent." Bergman couched her praise in the assessment that "she's too adorable."

Hawn continued to surprise everyone connected with *Cactus Flower* as those all-important early dailies began to come in. The producers and director were astonished to find that Goldie, through flawless timing and believable delivery, was stealing every scene she had with Bergman and Matthau. And she was doing it without the use of her trademark giggly *Laugh-In* voice. "Of course, if I got excited during a scene, it [her voice] did go up again," she said chuckling.

In a hilarious disco dance sequence that featured Hawn, Bergman, Matthau, and Jack Weston, her instinct was in top form as she countered dance movements and snappy dialogue without missing a beat. Continual praise made her confidence begin to soar as the film neared its completion. "I found that movies just seemed to go better with my own personal chemistry than does television," she remarked during a postproduction interview.

It was comments like that and the early buzz on her performance in *Cactus Flower* that foreshadowed her departure from *Laugh-In*. Goldie returned to the show for the 1969–70 season but felt torn between the potential of big-screen success and the security of the small screen. "I knew I had grown during the time I had been away from the show. Going back to *Laugh-In* was, in a way, a strange experience."

Adding to Goldie's internal conflicts was the reemergence of her desire to lead a normal life. She confided to her mother that she was tiring of the Hollywood fast track. "She said, 'Mother, I don't want to be a star,'" Laura Hawn recalled. "She said, 'I want to have children.' I suggested that she might want to do both."

Ever the trooper, Goldie continued in top form during the second season of *Rowan and Martin's Laugh-In*. She had already advanced to the front line of performers on the show, and the new season's skits were featuring her more and more. Goldie was giving it her usual 110 percent, but it was evident that *Cactus Flower* had spoiled her for a long run on the show. Nevertheless, for the time being, she was content with the idea that she had emerged as *Laugh-In*'s true star.

Patti Hawn, during a visit in 1969, had a front-row seat to the magnitude of celebrity her younger sister had achieved. "My feelings about what had happened to her changed the first time I walked down the street with her. She was being recognized by people, and people were asking for her autograph. I was awed. My little sister was suddenly a celebrity. All the things I had taken for granted about her—her talent, her whimsy, her infectious giggle—had suddenly exploded. Although she had stayed the same and never changed, the nation had discovered her."

The *Laugh-In* executives sensed that Hawn was getting antsy and so began negotiations to extend her contract. Goldie was offered obscene amounts of money to continue to dance and say, "Sock it to me." She listened to the offers but refused to budge, wisely awaiting the release of *Cactus Flower* in 1969.

Cactus Flower opened to mixed but generally favorable reviews, with even the less kind notices extolling the virtues of Hawn and the fact that she had emerged as the true star of this slight comedy. Those were exactly the things she needed to hear.

Goldie quit *Laugh-In* in January 1970. She broke down as she made the announcement to the cast. She had a particularly heartfelt hug for Ruth Buzzi, with whom she had become very close. But the toughest moment came when she came face-to-face with the man who had launched her career, producer Schlatter.

"I bawled on George Schlatter's shoulder like a baby. It was really traumatic. I felt like I was breaking up my family and going away for good."

Once the tears dried, Goldie felt certain that she had made the right decision. "For me, it was the end of an era, the end of a part of my life. But I had the feeling that it was also the beginning of something that would be even more exciting."

5

Yeah...But Can She Act?

GOLDIE HAWN'S PLANE TOUCHED DOWN AT LONDON'S HEATHROW Airport on January 30, 1970. As she walked down the gangplank, her eyes went wide at the huge international press contingent that was snapping pictures and shouting questions at her. Some of the questions were typical fan-magazine fodder: "How does it feel to be married?" "Are you planning on having children soon?" There were also questions that cut to the heart of the film industry's indecision about Goldie Hawn, and the actress could easily envision the headlines that would result from her responses to them: "Can the Dumb Blonde Really Act?" The jury was still out.

Cactus Flower proved that Goldie was capable of much more depth than she displayed on *Laugh-In*. But even her best notices never strayed far from the fact that her Toni was cut from the same comedic cloth as her television alter ego and that such a "stretch" while significant, did not indicate that Hawn had suddenly emerged as a full-blown actress.

Her success in *Cactus Flower* did result in other offers. Shortly after she said, "I do," to Gus Trikonis and *Cactus Flower* was completed, she said okay to another acting opportunity, possibly opposite Peter Sellers, in the comic romp *There's a Girl in My Soup*.

The film, an adaptation of the moderately successful stage play

47

by Terence Frisby, featured Sellers as a middle-aged sex fiend who met his match in an innocent nineteen-year-old American girl. Goldie's first impression of this very British, very lightweight script was that it was merely a vehicle for her to charm her way through another insignificant role. What ultimately sold Hawn on the script was that her character, amid the fluff, paints a picture of someone who is wise beyond her years. Goldie felt that doing the film would drive home the point that she was indeed not dumb.

Unbeknownst to Hawn, there were some behind-the-scenes concerns regarding her potential costar Peter Sellers, whose large salary and reported erratic behavior had sunk his previous film, *Casino Royale*, and who was considered damaged goods in many quarters. Producer Frankovich, after much hand-wringing and concern that Sellers could easily "unbalance the film," hired Sellers at a much reduced salary.

Predictably, the gossip pages ran wild with speculation that Sellers, a notorious womanizer, had fallen instantly and deeply in love with his costar right under the nose of her unsuspecting husband.

"Did he fall in love with me?" Hawn speculated after filming concluded. "I don't really know. I know we got along real well. He was someone I found to be very complicated, very inspiring, and very, very funny. He had a marvelous sense of humor on the set. There were times when we were laughing so hard that we had to break for lunch....He was a fine, delicate, neurotic spirit."

Sellers dodged the question of a budding romance with Hawn, though he did indicate that he, like many of Goldie's costars, had had a wonderful working experience with the young actress. "She is so nice in the fullest possible meaning of the word."

Meanwhile, Goldie once again went to bat for Trikonis's still-undiscovered directing talents and landed him the job directing of a promotional feature for the film. Hawn seemed to have no problem with the fact that, to the community at large, her husband was once again riding her coattails. Trikonis seemed to have no problem with his wife's getting him work.

Hawn took the announcement that she had been nominated for

a Best Supporting Actress Oscar for *Cactus Flower* in stride. She was too busy working on *There's a Girl in My Soup* to return to the States to attend the ceremonies, and besides, the realist in her felt that she didn't have a ghost of a chance. "I was competing against all these great people. So I went to bed the night before the Academy Awards figuring, 'What's the use?'" Hawn was up against Dyan Cannon, Sylvia Miles, and Susannah York.

The telephone rang in Goldie's hotel suite at 6:00 A.M. on February 16, 1970. "I just looked over at the clock on my bedside and thought, What idiot is calling at 6:00 A.M.?" The idiot turned out to be her agent, Art Simon, who was calling with the news that she had won the Oscar for Best Supporting Actress. Hawn was initially excited but then subdued in discussing the award, the culmination of a three-year, "meteoric" rise from obscurity to stardom.

"I wanted to win for working hard. I like to sweat. That role was just a drop in the bucket. I felt winning the award was a bit of a deceit. I always thought you had to work for years and years to win an Academy Award, and I didn't."

The talent that had resulted in Hawn's Oscar nod had carried over into her current project. Director Roy Boulting quickly added his voice to the Goldie Hawn cheering section. "She has an instinctive and immediate understanding of what is required of her in this role," he reported during filming. "She has a real sense of timing and talent."

There's a Girl in My Soup's uneventful ride was about to come to an end. Goldie was caught off guard the day director Boulting came up to her on the set and said he would like her to play an upcoming bedroom scene with Sellers in the nude. The actress was shocked.

"We were well into the film schedule when I learned I was expected to strip...like, strip nude! Well, that was out! There was nothing about nudity in my contract, and so I refused to play that scene in the nude."

Boulting, in his gentlemanly English manner, persisted. He offered to clear the set of nonessential personnel and played on the young actress's insecurities by insisting that she should trust his judgment. The moral side of Hawn stood firm. She dug in her heels at the idea of being naked in front of the camera. When Boulting would not back down, Goldie went to producer Frankovich and protested doing a scene in which she would get out of Sellers's bed and appear momentarily, nude.

Hawn, looking back on the incident, insisted that she did not want to be perceived as "a bitch or somebody who would stomp off the set," so after some soul-searching, she agreed to a compromise scene in which she and Sellers would be seen moving around under the bedsheets but that she would not be seen in the nude. "I was satisfied with the compromise and felt good that I didn't give in just because I was so young and inexperienced."

Goldie returned to the States following the completion of *There's a Girl in My Soup* and settled into married life with Gus. With her business commitments behind her, another side of Goldie began to emerge. Before they were married, Hawn and Trikonis had been regulars on the party circuit, enjoying the novelty of going places and being recognized. But now they were quite happy to become homebodies. Goldie was finding purpose in such simple pleasures as knitting, cooking, reading, and making her own clothes. Hawn could have easily hired servants to take care of the couple's needs, but she steadfastly refused to make any glamour concessions in her private life.

"We stopped making the Hollywood scene and don't belong to any particular social circles," she proclaimed of her anti-Hollywood lifestyle. "Nobody really knows me in Hollywood. But to be perfectly honest, I don't think either Gus or I ever really liked the parties and that lifestyle that much to begin with."

Goldie continued to dance a fine line in her relationship with Gus. Trikonis's attempts at getting his directing career off the ground were still making little headway. He began to paint. The reality remained that while her husband was trying to find himself, Goldie was bringing in all the money. It was a situation that was never far from Goldie's thoughts.

She was familiar with the hurtful comments about "Mr. Goldie Hawn." She also knew that while he rarely brought up the subject of money, Gus's ego was taking a beating. The flood of press interviews inevitably got around to that topic, and Hawn would do her best to downplay the difference in Gus's and her earning power.

"Who makes what money and who has how much success will never make any difference to us because we have a mature relationship," Hawn repeated almost by rote during a number of interviews in the early seventies. "Gus and I are two separate human beings with separate feelings and goals."

Goldie would always praise her husband's talents and offer predictions in hopeful tones that "he was going to be an amazing director someday." Reporters would listen intently, not believing a word of it, and then go away and write about how Goldie was upset that she was making all the money. She would continue to put up a confident front in respect to the question of money, but her armor would sometimes crack.

Hawn exploded one day when a reporter had seemingly beat the money question to death but continued to harp on it. "It's so crazy! What difference does it make who earns the money? We share it, and we try to share the joy in what we use it for. It takes a lot of strength because we don't live in a void. People are always asking us about the money thing. Everybody's curious."

When money was not intruding on Goldie and Gus's relationship, there was the equally unsettling question of children. Goldie was ready to get pregnant and make lots of babies. It became a regular topic of conversation that usually ended with Trikonis putting his foot down.

"Goldie wanted to have children very badly," he related, "and I wouldn't let her. I just didn't feel we were ready to start a family. I couldn't have supported them properly, and I felt it was very important for me to do my fair share financially."

Hawn took a self-imposed hiatus from work throughout the remainder of 1970, turning down lots of offers, continuing to toy with the idea of having children, and watching on the sidelines as *There's a Girl in My Soup* opened to mixed reviews and good box office. Goldie was delighted that critics singled her out for a spirited performance, natural comedy skills, and a wide-eyed innocence that made her the perfect counter to Sellers. But the actress was also candid in expressing her disappointment at certain compromises made in the film's story line.

"Peter and I had great arguments with the director about the fact that my character left him at the end. I felt she was too tough on him and that it did not fit in with the tone of the rest of the film."

Her lack of input in those situations and the growing sense that she had little control over her own career led her to attempt to renegotiate the financial aspect of her four-picture deal at Columbia. Frankovich bluntly told her a deal was a deal and would not renegotiate the contract, which still had two pictures to run. But while tied to the contract, Goldie began making noises in the direction of getting the most out of the final two films. "I've had enough comedy," she told a reporter. "I need to get my teeth into something more substantial."

It was old-home week when Goldie made a return appearance on *Laugh-In* shortly after winning the Oscar and hammed it up with her old pals in some classic bits. That same year, Goldie showed her strong sense of loyalty when she agreed to do an exaggerated bump-and-grind and a hilarious striptease sketch in a George Schlatter–produced television special called *Burlesque Is Alive and Well and Living in Burbank*.

Therapy continued to play an important role in Goldie's life. Through the sessions, she continued to gain a clearer perspective on Goldie the traditional woman with traditional values and Goldie the celebrity who was living by a different set of rules.

Her feelings about Trikonis and the disparity in their incomes and levels of success were another matter. Part of her was comfortable with being the breadwinner in the family. The traditional woman in Goldie Hawn was crying out to be taken care of. "I had married an older man whom I then proceeded to fashion into a father figure," she stated in a rare bit of candor. "I was his little girl. But one day the little girl grew up."

Hawn ended her vacation in January 1971 when she traveled to Hamburg, Germany, to film the lighthearted caper film *$*, opposite Warren Beatty. The movie, in which Hawn would play Dawn Divine, the prostitute-friend who teams with bank employee Beatty to rob a German bank, seemed like a step away from the fluffy characters she had played in her two previous films.

Director Richard Brooks, who also wrote the script, came to the project with an enviable list of commercial hits, a mania for actual locations, and an unorthodox approach to filmmaking that seemed the perfect creative foil for Hawn. Warren Beatty had already established himself as a bankable superstar with a reputation for being able to spot up-and-coming talent. And so his statement that "he chose Goldie [for the film] because he believed in her talent" came as a strong recommendation.

Goldie entered the project with the usual butterflies but with a new business savvy. She saw $ as an opportunity to burn off the third picture in her Columbia deal. And she was aware that her agent, Art Simon, had of late become increasingly insistent that his charge do another film. Finally, Goldie had to admit that $ seemed like a safe box-office bet. "I thought it was going to be a big picture. It smelled like a hit."

Feeling the sting of reports of her lobbying for work for Gus on her previous films, Goldie did not make any attempts at getting her husband a job on $, and none was offered. Goldie, acting on selfish impulses for the first time in a long time, felt she needed some time alone.

In the meantime, her enthusiasm for $ had grown. She particularly liked the idea of being out and about in Germany and so took a crash course in the language just days before she arrived there. Her newfound proficiency in German served her well; she was able to converse like a local in Hamburg's antique shops and restaurants during her time away from the $ set.

The film turned out to be a trip into the twilight zone. Director Brooks was living up to his reputation as an unorthodox filmmaker. He insisted that the actors not see a completed script and would only distribute the necessary pages for the next day's scenes the night before. The film suffered a near-fatal setback when Beatty fell from a train during filming and was bedridden for two days.

For Goldie, $ was a test of both her acting and physical endurance. Brooks was a stickler and would do repeated takes of even the least significant scenes. His style of directing proved an education for Hawn who, in her previous films, had worked with predictable, by-the-book directors. A suspenseful scene inside a bank vault would prove to be an acting highlight for Hawn, as was a physically taxing chase sequence across a stretch of ice.

The on-screen chemistry between Beatty and Hawn was quite real. In fact, the dailies looked so good that the inevitable rumors of an offscreen romance between the on-screen couple began to circulate. Goldie agreed that Beatty and she were getting on famously but not romantically.

"We did become fast friends on that film," she said of the relationship that would survive infrequent get-togethers and periods of no contact at all. "I looked upon him as a crazy older brother. I think we got along so well because our characters are alike in...oh, so many ways. But the big reason why we got along so well was that Warren was the first man who told me I was really smart. I was twenty-six, and I had never heard that before. Warren telling me that gave me a lot of confidence."

Jean Simmons, Goldie's costar in $, took an immediate liking to the young actress, describing her as an outwardly friendly and genuine person. "She's just as one would have hoped she would be."

Hawn returned to the United States after the film's completion and turned on the happy talk when questioned about the shoot. But in the same breath, she also hinted that she was not completely happy with some of the director's choices regarding her character and with some of the inconsistencies of the story line that she discovered during the filming. While awaiting the release of $, Goldie went looking for something less stressful and closer to home for her next project and found both in an offer to do her first prime-time television special, *Pure Goldie*.

Pure Goldie, produced and written by her former *Good Morning World* bosses Bill Persky and Sam Denoff, was a lightweight mix of singing, dancing, and sketch comedy that included such guest stars as *Laugh-In* buddy Ruth Buzzi, Kermit the Frog, and in a sentimental musical moment, Goldie's father, Edward Hawn. Many critics cast a suspicious eye at Hawn's continuing to step back into the cocoon of television. Goldie saw the special, complete with vintage Goldie sight gags and a medley of songs by the Beatles, as a fun, almost childlike break from what she perceived as the more serious business of moviemaking, in particular the looming specter of *$*, which would open not too long after *Pure Goldie* aired in the summer of 1971.

"It was a total bust," lamented Hawn not too long after *$* opened to almost unanimous bad press. "I didn't like my character or what I did with her. It was a totally unthought out, unconscious performance. I can't even look at the picture. I've seen it one and a half times, and that's because, midway through the second time, I had to turn it off."

Hawn's assessment of her performance as "being just too silly" was echoed by a number of critics, who not only slammed the film but were quick to dismiss Goldie's efforts as a bad case of overacting. Licking her wounds, Hawn began making noises about producing, citing *$* as an example of actor as pawn. "You're an actor, an object, an instrument. Until you learn for yourself what's right and what's wrong, you listen to everybody but yourself. In that position, it's very easy to be seduced by a director, and then later you say, 'Why did I do that?'"

The post-*$* period continued to force certain pressures on Goldie. The tug-of-war between celebrity and normalcy could still cause moments of doubt. Therapy continued to help her, but it seemed to be sending Gus off into radically new directions as he fought a losing battle with his own self-worth. The most challenging of her husband's turns came when Trikonis began philosophizing on the concept of open marriage.

Trikonis, perhaps using the concept as a subconscious bludgeon against Goldie's wealth and stardom, would talk up the idea of being married but being allowed to be with others. Goldie initially balked at the idea, but Gus persisted, and so Hawn eventually began to publicly soften her stance on the subject.

"I could very well envision a person being satisfied by someone other than his or her mate and I wouldn't see it as being so threatening," she declared. "Gus and I have talked, and we've come to the conclusion that we could probably not go through life without one of us falling in love with someone else. I can't say the love between Gus and I will last forever. If it turns out that one of us meets somebody that they love more, then we'll go with that person."

While espousing the open-marriage line, Goldie maintained fidelity to Gus. Rumors surrounding the fragile state of their marriage began to emerge, the most destructive being that Trikonis had taken his newfound philosophy to heart and was engaging in at least one ongoing affair with Goldie's knowledge. Those stories were never proved, but Goldie would later admit that "Gus would hurt me from time to time."

The truth was that the marriage was breaking down over the issues of money and celebrity. Goldie painfully recalled the telltale signs. "He began to assume a more possessive attitude about my work," she remembered. "He would question why I was taking a particular project and why I was spending so much time away from the house. It was like suddenly he had forgotten the struggle I had had to get to where I was in my career."

Goldie stubbornly continued to hold on to the hope that Gus and she might weather the storm and be a family for all time. She regularly told interviewers that she would "love nothing better than to be unemployed and pregnant." But that was just a dream, and Goldie later recalled the conversation she had with Trikonis that, in her own mind, seemed to seal their fate. "One day I said to Gus, 'I wonder if we will stay married.' He said 'If we don't, it will be because we don't want to.'"

Goldie, still smarting from her first negative reviews in *$*, took the relatively easy step of choosing *Butterflies Are Free* as her next film role. The movie, which also starred Edward Albert and Eileen Heckart, was yet another adaptation of a Broadway play in which a young blind man and his overprotective mother find their way into the real world thanks to the intervention of a sexy, amoral, and totally honest actress named Jill. The role of Jill became an important step in the evolution of Goldie as a legitimate actress. To this point, Goldie had seemed to slide through the critical minefield on natural talent, charisma, and the physical skills she had learned as a dancer.

While she initially saw Jill as "an easy role to play," she changed her tune once filming began and immediately found new respect for the part she was playing. "Jill is turning out to be the most wonderfully written character and the most beautifully written relationship I've had in a film to this point. I'm looking forward to going to work each day."

Much of her enthusiasm centered on director Milton Katselas, the kind, gentle, but firm hand Goldie was seemingly in need of at that point. He succeeded in tapping into the actress' insecurities during filming and in the process broke her of an ongoing performance habit. Goldie would often fall back on *Laugh-In* mannerisms, eye rolling and giggles, when she was feeling uptight or insecure on a film set. "I found it surfacing quite a bit, and I didn't like it because I realized that when I would roll my eyes and do those other *Laugh-In* kinds of things, I was feeling really insecure, didn't know what I was doing or saying, and was not putting any real thought into my work."

Katselas had the cure for the problem. No matter how well a scene was going, every time Goldie would roll her eyes, the director would yell cut. After countless takes, Goldie got the point. Consequently, the sharp-eyed viewer of *Butterflies Are Free* was hardpressed to find an eye roll in the film.

Hawn was pleased with the completed film. She was drawn to the fact that in Jill she had some of the sharpest dialogue in a film to date and that she could effectively project cynicism in a believable manner. Hawn felt that she had finally turned the corner and could no longer be denied the title of actress.

With some downtime and as more of a lark than anything else, Goldie decided to test her long-dormant singing skills by doing an album of country-and-western standards called *Goldie*. She knew the history of glorified vanity projects by movie and TV stars who can't sing a lick but felt that she had the singing skills to not embarrass herself.

The recording session, which included the talents of the

legendary Buck Owens and the Buckaroos, was wall-to-wall fun, if a bit overorchestrated and overproduced. Goldie was fair as a singer, although Dolly Parton had nothing to worry about. Unfortunately, Goldie and its one single ("Uncle Penn" backed with "Butterfly") failed to hit the charts. The album's producer, Andrew Wickham, said, "We were ahead of our time. If we had that record out five years later, it would have been much more successful. Goldie has a wonderful voice, and she was a joy to work with."

Butterflies Are Free was released in mid-1972 to critical and box-office success. Critics agreed that Goldie could indeed act. But Goldie felt that there was little time to savor the success. With her personal life in shambles, she immediately threw herself into her next professional challenge.

For Goldie Hawn, the question remained: Could she top herself?

6

Shattered

GOLDIE HAWN WAS HAPPY. BUT AS SHE CLOSED IN ON HER twenty-seventh birthday in late 1972, she could have been happier.

She was receiving the accolades, and the well-into-five-figures salary she was getting was commensurate with her arrival as one of Hollywood's top attractions. But Hawn was not happy with the scripts that she was seeing in the wake of her success. Most offered retreads of the kinds of characters she had portrayed in *Cactus Flower* and *There's a Girl in My Soup,* an indication that nobody was all that impressed by her performance in *Butterflies Are Free.*

And then there was the growing dissatisfaction with her manager, Art Simon.

Simon was pushing Hawn to work, and with the distractions mounting in her personal life, Goldie definitely wanted to stay busy. But she fretted that Simon seemed more interested in getting his 25 percent than in steering her toward any meaningful roles. "When he first became my manager, I adored him. "But then he started using me as a power tool. I was beginning to feel that I wasn't being represented properly."

Hawn was at her lowest when the script for *The Sugarland Express* was delivered to her doorstep. *The Sugarland Express,* written by Hal Barwood and Matthew Robbins, is based on the true story of a young, illiterate backwoods woman, Lou Jean, who takes matters into her own hands when the state threatens to take her son away from her and put him up for adoption. Lou Jean, as the story unfolds, breaks her jailbird husband out of prison, kidnaps a policeman, hijacks a police car, and leads law enforcement on an action-packed race across Texas.

In Hawn's eyes, Lou Jean, with her alternately cunning, comedic, and dead-on serious turns, had all the makings of the breakout role she was seeking.

"She was the definitive character," the actress opined as she sized up the script. "She was somebody you just wanted to gobble up. She was driven, controlling, and not a very nice person. She didn't give a shit about anybody but her child. I felt I would have no trouble playing her."

Even Simon, who was inclined to have Goldie do *Cactus Flower* clones until the cows came home, agreed that *The Sugarland Express* would allow Goldie to turn the corner into meatier roles.

Hawn's interest was met with shouts of joy at Universal Studios. *The Sugarland Express* was one of those scripts that had been silently making the rounds of studio heads for quite some time. The consensus was that it was the prestige, potential-Oscar-caliber film that Universal desperately needed and one that could be made on a relatively small budget. And it definitely needed star power in the lead because Universal was going to entrust the film to a talented but basically untried director: Steven Spielberg.

Spielberg, on the strength of a spine-chilling television movie called *Duel* and solid work directing episodes of *Night Gallery* and *Marcus Welby M.D.*, was considered the fair-haired boy who had come to deserve his first theatrical-level shot, and *The Sugarland Express* seemed the ideal project. But Universal would not green-light the film without a name actress to guarantee some marquee value. Hawn's participation was a name that would get people in the seats.

Goldie boarded *The Sugarland Express* in December 1972. She wanted the part so badly that she agreed to do it for only a fraction of her normal fee, $300,000 plus 10 percent of the profits.

Simon bit his lip. But sensing her dissatisfaction with his

management style, he felt that throwing her this bone might help keep her in his camp.

A meeting with Spielberg confirmed the fact that Hawn and he wanted the same thing out of Lou Jean's character: a top-flight dramatic performance. The fledgling director, who admitted beforehand that Hawn's dramatic skills were a question mark to him, came away from the meeting with newfound respect for her.

"I always thought she was a dramatic actress because I could tell that she took her comedy very seriously," related Spielberg. "So I met with her, and we had a great afternoon. You could tell she was thousands of kilowatts smarter than the people on *Laugh-In* had ever allowed her to demonstrate."

Filming commenced in Texas on January 8, 1973. From that first day, Hawn's choice to do the film seemed the right one. Goldie, dressed down in frumpy, dirty clothes and hair curlers, chewing gum and being, by turns, violent, profane, seductive, and heart wrenching, was making the most of a performance that was being played out on dusty roads and in dirty small towns.

Early on there had been concern that audiences would not be able to get past the fact that this was still everybody's cute little *There's a Girl in My Soup* bundle of laughs. But things went deathly quiet the day Hawn's character raised her voice and a gun in anger and threatened to blow a cop's brains all over the highway. One could believe her in the role.

"It was the most rewarding work I had done to that point," she reflected. "I think it was my finest performance."

Goldie was also making points with the cast and crew for her attitude in the face of long shooting days and nights on far-flung locations and under uncomfortable working conditions. She did not bitch when it was hot. She did not beg to go to her trailer when it was cold and dusty. Goldie was also in tune with Spielberg's vision of the film and, although still somewhat shy, would occasionally suggest how she thought a scene should be played. Spielberg was pleased with the fact that Goldie was not acting like a Hollywood starlet.

Typical of her adjustment to this more rough and tumble style of filmmaking was the day in a small Texas town when a shoot-out with the police in a used-car lot resulted in Goldie's getting shot with special-effects bullets and being around cars that were getting blown up. While a stunt double was on hand for the really dangerous moments, Goldie was quite intent as she huddled with the director and the special-effects chief, earplugs in place to blot out the noise. The first take of this complex sequence came off surprisingly well. Goldie managed to scream and twitch on cue as she ran through the hail of gunfire. As it turned out, the earplugs were not doing the complete job, and so the actress's screams turned out to be real and painful. Despite the ringing in her ears, Goldie willingly went through a number of takes before Spielberg was finally satisfied.

The action continued throughout the afternoon, with Goldie once again dodging gunfire as she leaped into a damaged car and struggled with actor Michael Sacks for control of a two-way radio. The crowded conditions in the car indicated that this scene was going to be tough to film. But a cheer went up after only two takes when Spielberg proclaimed, "Cut. Print it." While waiting for new camera angles to be set, Goldie, still wrapped around Sacks in the car, broke into a slightly off key rendition of the song "Everything's Coming Up Roses" that had the dusty Texas streets echoing with laughter.

As it turned out, everything was not coming up roses on the set of *The Sugarland Express*. The film was falling behind schedule and going over budget to the tune of the then ungodly sum of $50,000. Spielberg, it was feared, had gotten in over his head. The director, years later, would recall that a lot of the problems could be laid at the feet of Goldie.

"It was important for Goldie, because she had never played a consistently dramatic role before, to get it perfect," he remembered. "Consequently, we were shooting a lot of takes, and in the editing stage I would select the ones that were the most subtle and use those."

Too many takes, as it turned out, was not the only problem. As filming progressed, it became evident that the director and his star were not always seeing eye to eye. Their disagreements never got too heated, but one only had to look at the expression on Goldie's face to know that she was frustrated with some of the creative turns the film was taking. Spielberg was open to suggestions, but he had his own vision of the film, and it was a vision from which he was not about to back down. And so it came as no surprise that the actress was not thrilled when she saw the first rough cut of the film. "It was too serious, too unrelenting, and too uptight," she said.

Universal agreed. So while Spielberg reluctantly struggled in the editing room with a less dark approach, Goldie attempted to unwind and, in a last-ditch attempt to save her marriage, took her first real vacation in several years with Gus.

The time off appeared to energize the couple and their floundering relationship. They appeared happy and loving that spring when spotted in public. In reality, however, the vacation was a hellish personal encounter in which the pair laid all their emotional cards on the table and discovered that they were holding nothing in their hands.

The difference in their income and celebrity as well as Trikonis's continued resistance to having children had combined to push the marriage to the breaking point. Trikonis recalled a conversation during the last stages of their relationship that indicated the marriage was over. "Goldie tried her best to deal with it, but she also felt that she had to flex her own muscles. She said, 'I have to get on with what I'm doing.' And I said, 'Well, that's fine. I'll be around.' But it just sort of ended."

Goldie was torn. She was feeling guilt. She was feeling relief. She was feeling anger and sadness. And she was not sure whether any of these emotions was right or wrong.

Goldie threw herself into her work. There was no film project that struck her fancy, and so she accepted an offer to do a one-woman show for television in Las Vegas. The weeks of rehearsal for this singing, dancing comedy hour were just the tonic to take Goldie's mind off the end of her marriage. The special, complete with all the glitz that Las Vegas could muster, was a lighthearted romp that gave viewers a front-row seat to Hawn's growing prowess as an all-around performer.

With the show behind her, Hawn and Trikonis came to the conclusion that there was no use hiding the fact that their marriage was over, and in December 1973, Goldie announced that she and Trikonis were living apart and legally separated. It was to be expected that Goldie would diplomatically site pressures caused by divergent careers and time spent apart as the main causes of their breakup. Trikonis, his Greek pride hurt more than he was willing to admit, was not as charitable, placing the blame squarely on Goldie's shoulders.

"It was Goldie's career that broke us up. Things changed so quickly once she became famous on *Laugh-In*. Within a year we had moved from this little apartment in Hollywood to Bel-Air. She was getting all the phone calls and the attention, and I found that difficult to deal with. Goldie kept trying to reassure me, but I just couldn't see what she needed me for."

The breakup did not turn into the brawl that most Hollywood gossip columnists were expecting and secretly hoping for. Hawn and Trikonis simply went their separate ways. "We didn't get divorced," said Hawn. "Neither one of us wanted to remarry, so we just didn't see the point."

While she was outwardly relieved that the marriage was over, Goldie, in reflective moments, would concede that the breakup had taken its toll. "I felt I had pretty much drained my bucket. I just wanted to go somewhere and meditate. I did not want to work."

Her manager was not thrilled by that pronouncement. By this time Goldie was getting a minimum of $350,000 a picture, and Simon was getting 25 percent of that. It was in his best interest to keep Goldie working. Hawn and Simon went around and around about her working in the period after the separation. She insisted that she needed the time off. He insisted that working would be the perfect anecdote for her troubled personal life. Finally, it was the promise of a meaty role in *The Girl From Petrovka* that brought Goldie, in an admittedly ragged emotional state, back to work.

The Girl From Petrovka was a classically old-fashioned tearjerker about a Russian ballerina who falls in love with an American newspaper correspondent. Their romance unfortunately is doomed when it is discovered by the KGB. The film promised a solid cast that included Hal Holbrook and Anthony Hopkins, a director, Robert Ellis Miller, well versed in lavish locations and scope, and the opportunity to shoot on the streets of Russia. After agreeing to do the film, Goldie went to Russia for four days to research the part. Her enthusiasm for the project was soon dampened by the realities of politics.

The Russian government, which had initially agreed to allow filming, suddenly found some things about the script it did not like and withdrew its permission a week before the movie was scheduled to begin. The producers scrambled to find a substitute country and chose Yugoslavia. Then script problems developed, and there was a rush of rewrites. Just about the time the script became satisfactory, Yugoslavia revoked permission to shoot the film. Goldie reported that she "was getting upset by the delays."

Adding more misery to Goldie's life was the fact that, twelve months after its completion and following what Spielberg angrily reported as "twenty-eight mediocre marketing campaigns" by the studio, *The Sugarland Express* was finally released in the spring of 1974. The movie and Goldie garnered good reviews, but in terms of audience reception, *The Sugarland Express* ultimately fulfilled Spielberg's premonition that it was "a doomed film."

Universal quickly designed yet another marketing campaign and a new poster of Goldie holding a teddy bear that, according to Spielberg, did more harm than good. "People saw that it was a Goldie Hawn film and that she was holding a teddy bear and thought it was a kids' film."

Despite his acknowledged conflicts with her during the making of the film, Spielberg jumped to Goldie's defense. "The film's failure was not due to the presentation of Goldie as an anti–*Laugh-In* character. It had nothing to do with Goldie being rejected by audiences."

Goldie put the best possible spin on the experience, even as *The Sugarland Express* was being branded a box-office disappointment. "It was a very heavy picture, one full moment after another. I look at it now as being my finest performance."

Goldie's feeling that *The Sugarland Express* had served the purpose of showcasing her as a serious actress was soon being echoed around Hollywood. Enough of the right people had seen the film to suddenly justify bringing up her name in casting conversations for other than comedic roles. Producer Julia Phillips, who had developed a friendship with Hawn, put it this way: "That film reestablished her as a name that it was okay to put on a B list of actresses when you're trying to cast a movie. She's a star. A star and a major actress."

In fact, Phillips thought enough of Goldie's bankability to offer her the title role in the film adaptation of the bestseller *Fear of Flying* that she was trying to get off the ground. Goldie read the book, liked it, and agreed to lend her name to Phillips' package that was making the rounds of the studios.

The producers of *The Girl From Petrovka* were finally able to secure Vienna as a stand-in for Russia, and the film went before the cameras on November 7, 1974. Goldie had a good time making the film. The chemistry among herself, the other actors, and the director was good. On her days off, Goldie was able to indulge her mania for antiques with huge shopping sprees in area shops.

It was also during the making of *The Girl From Petrovka* that Goldie succumbed to loneliness and had her first postseparation affair, with Swedish actor Bruno Wintzell. Wintzell was a pretty face, a good body, and not a real deep thinker; the relationship was just as superficial as Goldie needed it to be. The relationship lasted only as long as it took for Hawn to finish the film, but pictures of the pair together were proof positive that Goldie was not about to go into an emotional shell.

Once she returned to the States, it was not an uncommon sight to see Goldie out in public on the arm of any number of handsome men. Her most significant relationship, following her return from Vienna, was with stuntman Ted Grossman, but it seemed by design that Goldie was refusing to get serious with anyone. She admitted that she still had bitter feelings about the breakup with Trikonis and was not willing to throw herself into another serious romance at that point.

These were trying emotional times for Goldie. She would often appear at loose ends. She continued to confide in friends that she was lonely and that the desire to have children had become almost too much to bear. But in the same breath, she would vow that she would never marry again.

What she was willing to do was throw herself into her work. Turning this new page in her life meant, she decided, divesting herself of longtime manager Art Simon. It was not an easy decision to make. Simon, despite her recent misgivings, had done a lot for her—which made things doubly tough when she finally broke the news to him shortly after completing *The Girl From Petrovka*. Simon did not take it well.

He tried to talk her out of it by appealing to her sense of loyalty, citing how wonderful their professional relationship had been and, in a not too subtle manner, how he had brought her from obscurity to stardom. When that approach did not work, he took her to court.

According to Goldie, he sued her for $6 million. Simon was charging breach of contract and, owing to the vagaries and fine print common in Hollywood deals, appeared to have the letter, if not the spirit, of law on his side. Simon was making not too veiled threats of a long, drawn-out lawsuit. "It seemed like I was going to have to spend the rest of my life in court," Goldie said with a sigh.

The rigors of settling with her ex-agent put the kibosh on Goldie's plans to get away from it all. It was at that point, in the winter of 1974, that she was approached by Warren Beatty to be part of an ensemble in a film he was producing, had cowritten, and was starring in called *Shampoo*. As mounted by Beatty, *Shampoo* was meant to be the last satiric word on the anything-goes moral attitude of the 1970s. It followed the exploits of a California hairdresser and the many women in his life on an emotional voyage of self-destruction and self-discovery.

Beatty insisted that Goldie was perfect for the role of Jill, one of his character's more stable bedmates. Goldie was not sure. "I felt Jill was the least attractive character in the entire script. She was just totally uninteresting."

Beatty persisted, insisting that what she saw was just in the script and that once they strated filming, she would easily bring the character to life. He offered Goldie her normal fee of $300,000 as well as 7 percent of what he felt would be the film's assured profits.

And true to Beatty's words, Goldie, during filming, "really discovered this character. I was finding the things that made Jill work. As it turned out, I played the only character in the film that seemed to have any future. I played the traditionalist in a very untraditional film."

Hawn found that *Shampoo* was an arduous and often uncomfortable shoot, the main reason being that Beatty, with the dual pressures of producing and starring, had suddenly turned very demanding. Takes that she was happy with were often overruled by Beatty. His attention to even the most minute details of a scene, at the end of an especially rough day, became annoying. Goldie admitted that *Shampoo* put a strain on their relationship for quite a while after filming was completed.

"It was a tough experience," she remembered. "It wasn't easy working with Warren."

Shampoo did have its bright spots, the most memorable being the final showdown in which Beatty and Hawn's characters dissect the remains of their love and relationship. It was a riveting moment in the picture, and Goldie's real-life struggles made the scene cathartic and more a reflection of the real person than the character she was playing.

Real life was a hurdle that Goldie was dealing with on the set of *Shampoo*. Emotionally, her explosive scenes with Beatty seemed to be allowing the actress to work out some of her unresolved issues with Trikonis. The pure physical attachments in *Shampoo* mirrored the emptiness she was experiencing in her recent, fleeting relationships. It was obvious, according to those on the set who knew Goldie's history, that something more than acting was going on. How well the process was working for Goldie was anybody's guess.

Goldie had found a new agent, Stan Kamen, a comfortable fit, a low-key kind of pusher who was equally adept at finding creative as well as financial opportunities for his client.

Kamen and Julia Phillips found a major studio for *Fear of Flying* in Columbia Pictures, but talks were dragging because the studio executives were not ready to risk paying Goldie $300,000 plus a percentage of any profits on a film they considered a risky venture at best. Adding to the complications dogging the film was the insistence of producer Phillips, who suddenly fancied herself a director, that she direct the film. Goldie began feeling less and less enthusiastic about the film and finally backed out, but true to form, she remained friends with Phillips.

In 1974, around the time Beatty was wrapping *Shampoo*, *The Girl From Petrovka* was released. Unfortunately, the good vibes generated on the set did not translate into a very good movie. Critics savaged the film. Hawn was disappointed but by that time had developed a tough hide when it came to creative disappointments. "I wish it had gone through the roof, but it didn't. But then most movies don't."

Life after *Shampoo* remained a struggle. Goldie was still suffering some emotional aftereffects of the breakup with Trikonis. Subsequent relationships had let her know that she was still attractive to men, but she conceded that these flings were emotionally empty.

Scripts were piling up. Goldie felt that her life was stuck in neutral and that being around Hollywood and Hollywood types was not helping. She decided it was time to disappear for a while.

"I just took off," said Hawn. "I wasn't that anxious to get back to work, and there were just too many places that I wanted to see."

7

The Sweet and Sour Life

PATTI HAWN CAUGHT THE TELEPHONE ON THE SECOND RING. IT was Goldie. She wanted to know if her big sister had a few days to kill.

Patti, recently divorced from her husband and feeling as emotionally confused as her younger sister, was used to getting those kinds of calls. Since her self-imposed hiatus in early 1975, Goldie was regularly looking for company when she decided to make jaunts to Europe, New York, or back home to hang out with Mom and Dad. Sometimes Patti would go along. By all accounts, Goldie, in tandem or on her own, was enjoying the first stress-free period in a long time, sightseeing, enjoying the nightlife, and just hanging out and not doing much of anything.

Goldie and Julia Phillips still maintained a close friendship despite the fact that they could never click professionally, and so Hawn, when she was in town, would party with her. Phillips recalled one night in 1975 when the two got together in New York to see the Rolling Stones in concert.

"Goldie is in jeans, a shirt, and a flak jacket," described Phillips. "Her hair falls in tendrils out of a makeshift ponytail. She looks just right to go to this concert." The pair were driven to Madison Square

70

Garden and were ushered backstage to meet the band. Phillips remembered that Hawn was "all giggles. The best thing about running with Goldie is the giggle."

Even while caught up in the rock-and-roll decadence and rubbing shoulders with Mick Jagger and Keith Richards, Goldie maintained her standards and morals. When a backstage hanger-on offered Goldie a sample of rock cocaine, she turned it down. Phillips, recalling the incident, saw it as establishing her own set of ethics and rules. "It said, 'This is not a coke whore.'"

Through the grapevine, Goldie would hear that Trikonis was getting on with his life, seeing other people, beginning to get a toehold in Hollywood, and making no moves toward a formal divorce. Goldie, as was her style, was happy for Trikonis and wished him luck with the rest of his life.

Litigation with Art Simon continued to drag on until Goldie finally threw up her hands and agreed to an out-of-court settlement. "I finally settled for a small fortune," she reported, "but it was worth it. I bear Art Simon no ill will, but I'm thankful that he's finally out of my life."

Goldie was also keeping tabs on *Shampoo,* which had recently opened to mixed reviews and so-so box office. She felt that *Shampoo* would either be loved or hated and so she took her good notices and moved on. In fact, the only thing Goldie was concerned with as her plane taxied down the runway, headed from New York to Los Angeles on the final leg of yet another 1975 jaunt, was how to get her seat belt fastened before the plane lifted off. In frustration, she looked to the occupant of the seat next to hers for help and found that he was having the same problem.

The handsome man smiled at her and shrugged. They joked and laughed at the absurdity of their situation as they finally managed to get their belts buckled just as the plane lurched into the sky. Hawn immediately sensed a kindred spirit in the man who introduced himself as Bill Hudson.

It's easy to understand why Hawn and Hudson hit it off. "I could see that he wasn't your normal Hollywood frightened person," she said of her first impressions. "He wasn't your normal Hollywood manipulator. I could see that he was true and honest, a very good person."

Hudson, whose given name is Salerno, grew up in a less-than-ideal family. His father dropped him off at school on his first day of kindergarten, left town, and was never seen again, leaving the family, which included two younger brothers, to grow up on welfare. What tugged at Goldie's heart was his positive attitude, through it all, toward family. Hudson meant it when he said, 'When you grow up cared for and yelled at by an Italian family, you grow up loved."

"We just started talking," recalled Goldie of that fateful flight to Los Angeles, "and we hit it off right away. By the time we were due to land in Los Angeles, he had asked me to have dinner with him."

Dinner was a low-key but joyously eye-opening experience. She discovered that Bill was a part of the popular recording group the Hudson Brothers. He regaled her with tales of touring, recording, and their coming big break as a summer replacement series for *The Sonny and Cher Show*. That he could make her laugh was a plus in the early stages of this dating game. So was the fact that he was not overwhelmed by her celebrity.

"Dinner was so wonderful, so warm," she recalled. "By the time we were finished, my head was spinning. I wasn't in love at that point, but I was sure our friendship was going somewhere."

Hawn and Hudson were soon inseparable. And it was not long before her initial impressions about him as a potential life partner were confirmed.

"Almost immediately after we met, we began talking about children. I felt he would be a wonderful father. Bill comes from a family that is real loving and warm. He has known deep love and affection. This was important to me because I knew he would be capable of giving that kind of love to his children."

Rejuvenated by this new relationship, Hawn soon found the old emotional fire and turned her attention back to her professional life. Aided by the sharp-eyed Kamen, she attacked the latest batch of offers with an eye toward something new, different, and most of all, funny. Her instincts were particularly aroused by a script called *The Duchess and the Dirtwater Fox.*

This strictly-for-laughs film, following on the heels of the message-oriented films *The Sugarland Express* and *Shampoo,* seemed an odd choice and a step back into stereotype for Hawn. But the role of an Old West dance-hall girl who teams up with a bumbling cardsharp was very appealing to Goldie.

"To be quite frank, I really pictured this as a part for Glenda Jackson," said writer-director Mel Frank, "but when she could not do it, I thought, Why not use an American girl who pretends to be English? Goldie seemed the perfect choice."

"I decided to do it because it was pure entertainment," Hawn said of her choice. "I would finally be able to do what I was trained to do, which is sing and dance. I also wanted to do a picture with George Segal."

In preparation for the film, Hawn had to be believable in an Old West setting and so she willingly threw herself into learning how to ride a horse and handle a gun. "It was fun. It was like playing."

Goldie continued to play once she arrived at the film's Colorado location in February 1976. Bill made a couple of visits when his schedule permitted, and Goldie's mother flew in for a week. When her father offered that he could only stay a couple of days, she made it possible for him to not have to rush back to work by wrangling him a small part in the movie.

Goldie was still very anti–show business when it came to dealing with Hollywood perks. Consequently, she got quite upset when the studio put her in a faceless, upscale hotel in downtown Denver. "The studio had me in some awful penthouse suite. It was just the most terrible place. They actually had an armed guard by my door. Well, I just packed my things, threw them into my car, and found this sweet little cottage right in the middle of town. The studio didn't think it was appropriate for a star. But I loved it."

On the surface *Duchess,* as advertised, appeared to be pure entertainment, with a tendency toward simplemindedness. But Goldie was quick to point out the challenges in playing a character like bar girl Amanda Quaid. "This is much more sophisticated comedy than I've ever done before. In most of my comedies I've played naive girls. In this one I'm more knowing, and that's more difficult than playing a soft girl. This one is tougher and stronger than her man, and she knows it."

Director Frank became an immediate convert to Goldie's sense of comic timing, telling anyone who would listen that "in the comedy department, nobody can touch her." Hawn described the film as "a symphony in which we all felt the same music."

While happy in her work, her relationship with Hudson was very much on her mind. In her wistful moments she was already looking to the future. "Sure there are other things I would rather be doing," she said one day during a break in filming. "I'd like to be having a child or lying on the beach in the Bahamas."

The relationship continued to blossom. They quickly became intimate in a natural, romantic way. But when Goldie turned up pregnant with Hudson's child four months after their first meeting, well, that was a total surprise.

"Now I'm happy," announced Hawn not long after going public with the news that she was pregnant. "I feel I can really appreciate this baby."

Despite every intent to marry Hudson, Goldie was not in any great rush to legalize their relationship. He was busy working on his television series, and Goldie would dismiss any questions of marriage by saying, "There's a lot of stuff going on."

Much of Hawn's "stuff" centered on her impending divorce from Trikonis and the fact that while she was still tending to keep her emotional cards hidden, she was still scarred. The idea of marriage had suddenly emerged as an ugly word that brought to Goldie only the still-fresh images of disappointment and sadness. Despite her reservations, she had finally begun divorce proceedings when she found that Trikonis was evoking California's community-property divorce laws in demanding spousal support from his soon-to-be ex-wife.

"I was hurt," said Hawn in response to Trikonis's demands. "He never supported me a day in his life. I don't believe he deserves it. I just don't understand how, if two people are capable of making a living, why they have to feed off each other."

As the weeks and months went by, Goldie began to balloon up from her normal 119-pound weight to what would eventually reach 170 pounds. Both Goldie's and Bill's professional lives had slowed to the point where they announced that they would be getting married as soon as Goldie's divorce was final.

"I think we're both the marrying kind. We hope to have lots of children," said a radiant Hawn, who had suddenly become a marriage advocate.

In the meantime, Goldie had, happily, begun her latest hiatus. The Hudson Brothers had finished their television commitments and, with record sales soaring, were now back on the road with their musical-comedy show. Goldie, in the early stages of her pregnancy, would often go along.

"It's great!" she said. "I get to see the small towns, the big towns, we travel by plane and by car. I love to be on the go with Bill. I'm seeing new places and meeting new people. Right now my whole life is centering around Bill, and I love it!"

The Duchess and The Dirtwater Fox marched into theaters during the early months of her pregnancy, and Goldie's spirits were buoyed by reviews that praised her performance as being funny and sexy. "This picture is entertainment. It's fun, it's an evening out, and God knows, there's not enough of that. It's an upper. You walk away from it and you feel great. I think it's very exciting to be a part of something like that."

Goldie hung back, watching in almost childlike awe as her belly grew. There were the expected mood swings and hormonal rages that go along with any pregnancy, but she seemed to ride the waves fairly well. A big part of the stress-free early months was attributed to the fact that despite being pregnant and unmarried, Hawn had avoided being the subject of sensationalist press.

"Nobody ever said anything about it," stated a relieved Hawn. "It was really something. I mean, I didn't think it was terrible, and my family didn't have a problem with it. But you never know how the press is going to react. But nobody in Hollywood chastised me or warned me that I was wrecking my career. If they had, I would have said, 'Okay, so I'm wrecking it.'"

When not on the road, Goldie and Bill enjoyed an idyllic existence in her Bel-Air home. They were looking to the future and had already authorized construction to begin on a home in nearby Malibu. Pregnancy was a wonderful time for them. They began toying with names. Oliver Rutledge for a boy and Tessie Jean for a girl were names high on the list. Goldie also began fantasizing about the child growing inside her. "I realized, almost from the moment that I got pregnant, that he was a boy. I even knew the hair color he would have."

The couple also continued to find out more and more about each other. In her disagreements with Trikonis, Goldie would often seethe long and privately, while Bill was somebody who would not let the sun set on an argument before it was resolved.

"We would have these wonderful arguments," said Hudson, "and then we would get it all out and worked out."

For most of her pregnancy Hawn just sat around, not doing much of anything. "Bill loved me pregnant," she said of that time, "and I was quite happy eating. But it was funny, the first time my mom came to visit and saw how big I had gotten, she immediately put me on Weight Watchers."

Well into her sixth month of pregnancy, Goldie was now anxious to have her divorce from Trikonis finalized so she could get on with her life. But Trikonis was being difficult, continuing to push his demands for spousal support and attempting to use Hawn's middle-class values against her: He knew that his ex-wife, despite her pronouncements to the contrary, would feel some shame in giving birth while still unmarried. He also felt that Goldie's erratic emotional state, intensified by the pregnancy, would cause her to cave in at some point.

Indeed, the court battle was beginning to cause stress in Goldie's life, which, her doctor warned, was not good for mother or baby. Consequently, in June 1976 the pair agreed to a settlement that would have Hawn paying her ex-husband a lump sum of $75,000 in exchange for the final decree of divorce.

There was real anger in Hawn as she signed the legal documents. But the bitterness soon left her, and she was more evenhanded in the assessment of the wreckage that was her first marriage. "All of us have our own way of reacting to anger and hurt. Perhaps that was Gus's way. I really don't know, as we never spoke. But I do know that I could not have been the only one who walked away from this feeling hurt. I hardly enjoyed giving up seventy-five thousand tax-free dollars. But if that's the price of freedom, it's cheap at twice the cost."

On July 3, 1976, Hawn, now eight months pregnant, and Hudson married in the backyard of her parents' Takoma Park home. In a rather quiet ceremony, witnessed by seventy-five of the couple's relatives and friends, Goldie and Bill exchanged vows in front of a rabbi and a priest to accommodate the wishes of their respective parents.

"It was a big wedding," said Hawn of her special day. "It was a fairy tale. My father gave me away. My sister was my bridesmaid. I walked down the aisle. I had the whole thing."

The whole thing for Goldie was not simply a matter of a ceremony legitimizing their relationship. Goldie, who had recently turned thirty-two, had suddenly found herself in a much better place emotionally. She now stated that she was in the ideal frame of mind to be married.

"I was a child when I made it as Goldie Hawn," she explained not too long after she married Hudson. "I was a child when I married. Today I am no longer a woman who is afraid of her success. The 'little me' now has her priorities screwed on straight. If Bill asked me not to work, I wouldn't. Within weeks of meeting him, I felt being with him was more important than working. What Bill and I have is a lot of love and friendship. Whatever success I might achieve as the public Goldie Hawn cannot affect this marriage."

The newly married couple retired to their recently completed second home, a Victorian house nestled on a bluff overlooking the ocean in Pacific Palisades, and awaited the birth of their child. Goldie was due any second but was showing no signs of going into labor. That fact, coupled with what he considered a massive weight gain for her small frame, caused Hawn's physician to express some concern about the chances of survival for both the baby and, in hushed tones, for Goldie. In any case, a normal delivery was looking unlikely, and Hawn readily agreed to a cesarean section.

In her tenth month, Goldie finally went into labor. With Hudson at her side, she entered Southern California's Cedars-Sinai Medical Center, and after a two-hour C-section procedure, Oliver Rutledge Hudson came into the world in September 1976, weighing in at a hefty eleven pounds.

Despite being drugged and in much pain immediately following the operation, Goldie was deliriously happy. "When I first saw Oliver, he was so beautiful, and I was so happy. He was like an extension of me. It was the most intense attachment I've ever known. It made everything I went through worth it."

Goldie's joy, however, would be short-lived.

Within a couple of days, Oliver came down with pneumonia and he was put on a respirator. Hawn, whose C-section and shaky health prior to giving birth necessitated an extended stay in the hospital, had to now contend with the heartbreak of watching her child's health go from bad to worse. "It was too scary. I didn't know what was going to happen," she painfully recalled.

Hawn was officially discharged from the hospital ten days after giving birth. It was only because of her exhaustion, combined with the urging of Bill and her doctor that she finally went home. But home, in those scary days, was barely a pit stop; she'd get a few hours sleep, very little to eat, and then spend every waking hour at Oliver's side as her firstborn fought for his life.

Word of her happiness and sudden ordeal had quickly hit the newswires, resulting in an army of photographers and fans staking out Cedars-Sinai around the clock in an attempt to snap a photo of the distraught mother coming or going or to offer sympathy. With Hudson's help, Goldie managed to avoid the press and fans through an elaborate series of disguises. Once inside, according to those privy to her comings and goings, Hawn and Hudson would sit for hours beside the respirator, making cooing noises, shedding tears, and offering up silent prayers.

The prognosis was not good. Newborns were particularly vulnerable to even the slightest of colds. Pneumonia was often fatal.

But Oliver Rutledge Hudson's breathing began to become less labored, more measured. His temperature began to stabilize. Goldie's prayers were answered: Her child was going to live. "He just had this real strong will to live," said a relieved Hawn shortly after bringing her child home. "It was a real storybook ending. I was never more happy than when I took him home."

The couple retreated to their Pacific Palisades home and began their new life as parents. Hawn was joyous at the idea of breast-feeding and puttering around the house. "During that first year I was like most mothers. I was lucky enough to be able to stay home and play hausfrau." The Hudson Brothers were still a top touring act, and there had been serious talk about a possible syndicated television show. But when Bill was not working, he was home, playing in the recording studio Goldie had built for him as a wedding present or, most importantly, being the attentive, loving, supportive father and husband Goldie had always felt he would be.

"I knew that he was going to be the kind of father who would give physical love to his children," she said. "He was going to be the kind of husband who would get up in the middle of the night to hold them and to be with them. He's a wonderful, wonderful father."

Hawn, for her part, had made the decision early in her pregnancy to be the perfect mother, and that meant taking a break from work. "I had made the decision earlier to turn down all pictures that were offered to me. But to be perfectly honest, I was not being offered the cream at that point, anyway. For the most part, what I've been offered has been ineffectual and trashy."

In all honesty, Goldie was not that upset that quality scripts were not coming her way. Like most new mothers, she was caught up in the warm, cuddly notion of motherhood and the feeling of being complete as a woman. "Being a mother has made me feel as if I've completed a female function, as if I've found a missing part of me. I'm totally committed to this little person's well-being. I feel utter joy."

Home and hearth were the total focus of Goldie Hawn's life

through the rest of 1976 and most of 1977. The one substantial offer that came her way was a part in the first *Superman* movie. She turned it down because it would have taken her to London and away from home. There was talk of having another baby and perhaps adopting other children.

A regular visitor to the couple's home was Bill's brother, Mark. He was often greeted by Goldie dressed in jeans and a sweatshirt, her hair unkempt and in unruly tangles. "She would greet you at the door looking nothing like a glamorous superstar," recalled Hudson. "Sometimes she would wear an old T-shirt that came down to her knees, a short skirt, no makeup, and old sandals. And Bill would be there in his Bermuda shorts and Hawaiian shirt. They weren't chic, but they sure were comfortable. They were living like a couple of bohemians. Goldie had forgotten about her career and was concentrating on being a wife and mother."

For Goldie, this period of domestic bliss was by choice. "I turned down several pictures because I didn't want to do them. I had a baby. I was remodeling my house. I just needed time out to fill up."

Goldie's big commitment to domestic life had a lot to do with Bill Hudson's ability to be successful in his own right and to change with the times. When the popularity of the Hudson Brothers as a touring act began to wane by 1977, the trio turned their attention to television and landed a syndicated variety show called *Bonkers!* Filming in London, *Bonkers!* seemed like the first big stumbling block to the couple's marriage. Goldie and Bill, however, managed to work it out. Hawn would travel on occasion to London to be with Bill. Hudson was regularly on a flight back home during breaks in production. Life seemed to be working quite smoothly. But there was also a growing sense of frustration.

As Oliver approached his first birthday, Hawn began to realize that she had been out of the public eye for nearly two years and that her last two films, *Shampoo* and *The Duchess and the Dirtwater Fox,* had not met with much critical and box office success. "I started to get itchy about going back to work," she admitted. "My career had not been flourishing by any means, and that was partly by choice and partly not. I was wondering exactly what I was going to do.

There didn't seem to be anything tangible to look forward to, careerwise."

By 1977, Chevy Chase had emerged as one of the leading lights in the groundbreaking television series *Saturday Night Live*. The early buzz was that his engaging personality and comic timing would make him a natural in movies. Chase believed his press clippings and by the fall of 1978 had left *Saturday Night Live* in search of big-screen stardom. He chose *Foul Play* as his coming-out vehicle. *Foul Play* was something Goldie knew all about.

The script had been floating around Hollywood for several years, and Goldie had taken an instant liking to it. "I liked the script so much that I tried to get it financed myself but could not. I didn't realize that I probably could have gotten it financed myself. I just didn't know how the process worked."

Foul Play told the very Hitchcockian tale of a plot to assassinate the pope in San Francisco that is broken up by an unlikely team: a mild-mannered librarian and a San Francisco detective. Equal parts comedy and action-suspense, *Foul Play* seemed the perfect starring film for Chase. And in the role of librarian turned heroine, there was more than enough comedy and spunk to interest an actress like Goldie Hawn.

Years later, Goldie's interest in *Foul Play* remained high. She was a big fan of Chase's brand of humor and saw the potential for this comedy coming across well on the big screen. There was a lot of action, which was appealing after her months of relative inactivity and represented a chance to show yet another side of her acting. That *Foul Play* would be filmed on location in San Francisco and on the Paramount lot in Los Angeles met her requirement of staying close to home.

What Goldie had not counted on was the short memories of studio executives. In fact, early in the negotiating process Paramount had little interest in Goldie, preferring Farrah Fawcett in the role. But when Fawcett became embroiled in a lawsuit with ABC television network and producer Aaron Spelling, she became damaged goods in Paramount's corporate eyes. Paramount then set its sights on Hawn.

However, as there had been rumors that Goldie had gotten fat during her self-imposed layoff the studio heads insisted on giving her the once-over before offering her the part. Hawn seethed over the overt sexism of the situation. She ultimately went along with their idea of an audition but filed away the embarrassment for future reference.

Goldie said yes to *Foul Play* in early October 1977 and by Halloween was standing in the middle of the rolling streets of San Francisco, waiting for director Colin Higgins to yell action. As with every Goldie Hawn movie of late, the big question on *Foul Play* was chemistry, especially as it pertained to Hawn's reentering the workforce and the first film pressures on Chase. Higgins, to his credit, eased Hawn into the role, more often than not punctuating corrections and suggestions with a smile or a joke that would be reflected in Goldie's face. It was also noted that Hawn and Chase had taken an immediate liking to each other.

"I like Chevy. He's fun to work with," Hawn reported. "Sometimes he talks without thinking, which is something I used to get accused of doing. But he's great. We're a great combination."

The feeling was mutual. "Goldie, in her own wonderful way, has it all covered," Chase remarked. "She's a natural actress, and she's definitely not a dingbat."

Never too far away from Oliver and his ever-present nanny, Goldie threw herself into *Foul Play*. She did the majority of her own stunts. When a scene called for her character to be hanging on for dear life on a spinning catwalk, fifty feet in the air, Goldie was there. And despite flashbacks from her New York car crash, Goldie was at the wheel during *Foul Play*'s thrill ride up and down the hilly streets of San Francisco.

"I could barely see through the lighting and the camera equipment mounted on the hood of the car," recounted Chase. "But I could see that Goldie was really terrified, and it really helped to make the whole scene much more believable."

Appearing in her first full-blown action film, Goldie was ecstatic. "This is a real movie movie," she enthused. "There's thrills, shocks, and a whole lot of laughs."

82

When not shooting a scene, Goldie would be at Oliver's side or visiting with any number of family members who happened to have dropped by the set. Bill also made extended visits, which, for Goldie, made the family picture complete. When her schedule permitted, she could be found shopping at San Francisco's more trendy stores.

Films are never trouble free, and *Foul Play* proved no exception. There were long days, occasional clashes of will, more takes than anybody wanted to shoot of an arduous scene in which Goldie and Chevy had to run up the stairs of the San Francisco Opera House, and a lot of what Chase recalled as "some mild chaos." And while she would sometimes get annoyed with the snags in the process, one would have been hard-pressed to see it in Goldie's face.

"Goldie would always maintain her composure," Chase reflected of life on the *Foul Play* set. "She would sometimes laugh at herself, but you never saw any fits or displays of temper. That just wasn't her."

Foul Play moved back to Los Angeles and the Paramount lot at year's end and continued to film through January 1978. Chase continued to be head cheerleader when it came to his costar. "She's a fine actress because she's so natural," he exclaimed. "She never went out of her way to be any different than she really is except to add whatever ingredient was needed to make a scene work."

During the filming of *Foul Play,* Hawn continued to be reflective of matters personal and professional. She had fulfilled one element of her personality when she had a child and formed a traditional family unit. The fact that she had recently entered her third decade of life was also very much on her mind. "The nice thing about being in my thirties is that I no longer give a shit about a lot of things that used to worry me. I'm a woman now. I'm not a girl anymore. And I'm not afraid anymore."

With the completion of *Foul Play,* Hawn returned to the role of wife and mother. Work had agreed with her and had, in fact, energized her entire being. She was even more determined to expand her boundaries as a performer and to use her clout as a star whose participation could guarantee a film's getting off the ground to her advantage. Hudson was well aware of the attitude change in his wife and sensed that something was not quite the same about the woman who had always professed family first.

"Goldie was on the comeback trail and did not want to fail," Hudson said. "Her priorities shifted when she started doing *Foul Play*. Our kid was sort of left out as a number two priority. I just couldn't believe I was seeing that."

What was troubling Hudson was not the renewed sense of professional purpose in Goldie. What he was unhappily seeing was the dark side of his wife: arrogance, selfishness, and disregard for anything that did not fit into her sense of progressing in a material sense. Goldie definitely had her mind back on her work.

"When I started, good roles for women were really hard to come by, so I had to fight for every decent role I could get," she said not long after finishing *Foul Play*. "Now it's a little easier for me, but I feel that I have to keep proving myself over and over again that I'm no longer a cute little go-go dancer in a bikini and body paint."

She also insisted that the reality that both she and Bill had careers was not going to result in her having a "neurotic Hollywood child on my hands." When Bill was scheduled to be in London for an extended period of time and Goldie was seeing no major studio scripts that struck her fancy, she found the perfect solution to keeping the family intact and satisfying her creative needs: a small art-house film called *Lovers and Liars* (a.k.a. *Travels With Anita*).

Lovers and Liars, on the surface a zany road adventure, actually had, at its core, a complex and bleak tangle of sexual emotions. It also offered the opportunity to film in Rome opposite Italian screen star Giancarlo Giannini and to be close to Bill, making the choice of this small film over yet another big studio picture an easy decision.

The film turned out to be a smart creative choice for Hawn. Under the direction of Mario Monicelli, Hawn was educated in a pure European style of filmmaking. It magnified seemingly small moments, played comedy in a broad, over-the-top fashion, and forced her to try harder in the film's claustrophobic, intimate scenes.

The film turned out to be the ideal working vacation in the summer of 1978. With Oliver never too far away, Hawn worked during the week. On weekends she would either hop a flight to

Goldie on the set of *Laugh-In* June 1972 (All pictures courtesy AP/Wide World Photos)

(*Above*) At a reception in
London in February 1970

(*Right*) Arriving for the world
premiere of *Cactus Flower*, in
which she makes her film debut,
on December 15, 1969

(*Left*) Zooming around on the set of *There's a Girl in My Soup* (1970), which filmed in London

(*Below*) Work on *There's a Girl in My Soup* stopped while costar Peter Sellers presented a bouquet of flowers to Goldie

(*Opposite*) In a scene from *The Girl From Petrovka* (1974), Goldie's character, Oktyabrina, sits in a Russian nightclub and barely holds back her tears as she learns that her protector, a Russian minister, is being transferred out of the city.

(*Right*) With costar Chevy Chase on the set of *Foul Play* (1978)

(*Below*) With costar Armand Assante during the filming of *Private Benjamin* (1980)

Goldie as Kay Walsh, the devoted navy wife left behind during World War II, in *Swing Shift* (1984)

(*Right*) Goldie and Kurt Russell playing a love scene in *Swing Shift*

(*Below*) With Wyatt at the screening of *Peter Pan* at Disney Studios in Burbank in July 1989 (Janet Gough)

With Kate and Oliver at the Hollywood Palladium for the Big Sister event in Goldie's honor in December 1989 (Scott Downie)

London or Bill would come to Rome. Goldie was happy. "I like being this balanced in my life. I like not having a neurotic Goldie on my hands."

The couple's approach to marriage was clearly defying the Hollywood odds, and a big part of keeping things together was keeping them separate. There had been talk early in the marriage of the couple's collaborating in some way. But Hawn and Hudson were clear that they would not do so in the immediate future. "It's healthy to keep our careers as separate things," Goldie explained. "I don't bring home my work, and neither does Bill."

But public perception of Hawn and Hudson's marriage, based more on the memory of her previous marriage to Trikonis than on the current reality, was hard to shake. To the public at large, Goldie was the star and the breadwinner. And Hudson did chafe at the phrase "Goldie Hawn and her husband, Bill." "Sure it bothers me. It makes me seem like just one of the many events in her life. It invalidates what we really have with each other, which is our love and our relationship."

Hawn completed *Lovers and Liars* in mid-1978 and returned to the States. She barely had time to settle back into the quiet life of wife and mother when she discovered that she was once again pregnant. She and Hudson were ecstatic at the prospect of enlarging their family. Goldie also saw the pregnancy as a time of emotional and professional retrenching. There were things she wanted to do, and now, she reasoned, was the time to start putting her ideas into motion.

Goldie had long harbored the idea of getting more involved behind the camera, where, she felt, all the important decisions were made. Five months into her pregnancy, she was approached by a former script editor, Nancy Meyers, with a story idea. It was something called *Private Benjamin*. After reading the story outline, Hawn was hooked.

"You write the damned thing," she said, "and I'll produce it."

8

Life on the Rocks

GOLDIE HAWN AWOKE FROM A RESTLESS NIGHT'S SLEEP WITH THE worst bout of morning sickness yet. She raced to the bathroom and threw up.

After splashing water on her face and making a feeble pass with a makeup brush to cover up her pale skin, Goldie pulled a maternity smock on over her eight months' pregnant body and moved to the kitchen, where she thought about attempting breakfast. But the thought of solid food made her gag and sent her hurrying back to the bathroom. She emerged, moments later, and moved slowly and uncomfortably toward the front door.

Goldie was off to a business meeting, and nothing was going to keep her from making it.

Hawn had been so convinced that *Private Benjamin* was money in the bank that she immediately formed a production company with Nancy Meyers called Cherry Alley Productions and had set her to work on the script. Now all she had to do was find the project a home.

Private Benjamin with Goldie Hawn attached, would have been considered a slam dunk by any studio. But Hawn, who was vocal about how she felt the film should be done, was finding her producing debut a hard sell. It was an experience she looked back on with some anger.

"In the beginning, they [the studio executives] would pat me on the head. To them I was still the cute little Goldie. But the minute I stood up and had something to say, I became the bitch."

One studio executive at Warner Bros., who went public years later on the condition of anonymity, recalled his first look at the *Private Benjamin* treatment and early draft of the script. "The script was so empty, so stupid, so nonsensical, that you had to question why anybody would want to make it."

Despite the rejections, Goldie pressed on, thanks, in part, to inspiration supplied long ago by her father. "My father used to marvel at my ability to turn a corner very quickly. That's what I want to do now. I want to act, to produce, and to keep turning those corners."

By November 1978, Hawn was also considering another, nonproducing project, *Best Friends,* a comedy based on the real-life experiences of writers Barry Levinson and Valerie Curtin, who are attempting to make their marriage work. With the continuing burden of pregnancy and the ongoing, often stressful attempts to sell a studio on *Private Benjamin,* Goldie added to her already full plate by agreeing to take a look at the *Best Friends* script.

"I liked the script. It was funny and it was honest, and honest comedies are not easy to find." Goldie's agent, Stan Kamen, also agreed that *Best Friends* would be in his client's best interest. "I think Goldie saw *Best Friends* as something the public would like to see her in," he said.

The *Best Friends* camp upped the ante when they announced that Norman Jewison, a director Hawn respected, had agreed in principle to do the film. However, the project had to be put on hold because of Goldie's pregnancy and the fact that the star and the director were currently knee-deep in other work.

In the meantime, Goldie was doggedly continuing her pursuit of a home for *Private Benjamin.* Columbia and Paramount had heard her proposal and were enthusiastic about the comic possibilities of a naive rich girl who leaves her sheltered life for the U.S. Army. However, they demurred at the idea that Hawn would star in the film only if she were its executive producer.

"I didn't plan on becoming a producer," she said. "I never said that my next career move would be producing. I only wanted to create better roles for myself, and I loved the idea of *Private Benjamin* so much that I felt it would be the perfect opportunity to finally control my own destiny."

Hawn parked her car on the Warner Bros. lot and waddled painfully into the executive offices. Another wave of morning sickness hit her. She excused herself and went to the bathroom, threw up, and went into the meeting without missing a beat. "I walked right into Warner Bros. and said, 'If I don't make it here, I'll make it somewhere else,'" she recalled. "I felt I had earned the right to say what I said at Warners by performing properly over a ten-year period and proving that my instincts about film projects were correct."

Warner Bros., while not offering as large a cash incentive as other studios, was enthusiastic enough about the project to agree to Hawn's terms, which included her producing the film. A deal was struck just days before Goldie went into labor and delivered a bouncing baby girl named Kate in June of 1979.

Shortly after the birth of Kate, Hawn took an office on the Warner Bros. lot, where she remembered: "I was recruiting, talking to directors and set designers, casting, and pulling all the elements together."

During the nearly yearlong development process for *Private Benjamin,* Goldie was never far from the needs of Oliver and Kate and vehemently deflected the notion that her involvement in the picture was causing her to lose touch with her family side.

"I have my priorities. I haven't had to give up one thing for another. I know where my cutoff marks are. When I'm home, my phones go off. I don't take business calls there. I don't want my children to have to compete with that. My children and my home life are very important to me, but I'm not forfeiting my life, my career, the things that I do. I've tried to combine them, and I'm finding that it can be done very, very easily. There's always the awful guilt about becoming so involved in your work that your children suffer. My children are not suffering."

Hudson continued to shine in the background, spending quality time with the children and acting totally supportive of his wife's endeavors. The reason he had so much time to be a house husband was that by the end of 1978 his career was on the skids.

Bonkers! had not been renewed after the first season, and the musical-variety bent of the Hudson Brothers had fallen out of favor. Hudson was confident that he would pull out of the slump. But the absence of work while Goldie's career was skyrocketing began to manifest itself in frustration and controlling behavior similar to that exhibited by Trikonis. Because Hudson kept his anxieties bottled up, Hawn, while aware of and sympathetic toward her husband's inactivity, did not realize the damage it was doing to their relationship.

Lovers and Liars was released in April 1979. The film, despite Hawn's presence, was seen in only a few theaters in major cities in the United States and Europe. It was favorably reviewed but largely overlooked and quickly disappeared.

Meanwhile Hawn was experiencing the frustrations of getting a project off the ground and learning why the process was called "development hell." Even the simplest elements of mounting a film were taking an inordinate amount of time, and Goldie was getting restless. When the opportunity to do a television special, *Goldie and Liza Together*, with longtime friend Liza Minnelli presented itself, Goldie jumped at it.

The two actresses had met in 1974 when Hawn was a guest at the wedding of Minnelli and Jack Haley Jr. They were both stars, and they discovered that they had similar personal attitudes. The two women would make the effort to find time in their busy lives to work together. Liza flew out to Hollywood to tape the special on September 15, excited at the prospect of working with Goldie for the first time.

Goldie and Liza Together was not the typical variety show. The highly structured story line was a behind-the-scenes look at the seven days it took to pull together a television show. It featured a variety of singing, dancing, and production numbers well suited to the talents of the two women. Highlights included Goldie, backed

89

by an all-male chorus, singing the song "YMCA" and she and Liza singing a medley of songs that included "One Step," "The Other Woman" and "All That Jazz." As production on the special commenced, the duo discovered that their work habits were well matched.

"Goldie and I are like two cartoon characters," said Minnelli. "She's the blond airhead, but she's really Einstein. I've worked with other women before, and it was tough, but working with Goldie was totally different. If there was something wrong with my dress, she would fix it. I know people who would have let me go on covered in lint. The basis of the show we did was to prove you don't have to be better than anyone else, you just have to be as good as you are."

As she and Minnelli were going through a rigorous rehearsal of dance routines and production numbers, Goldie did not know that her partner was pregnant. In fact, nobody knew, because Minnelli, a shy person with few friends in her nonprofessional life, did not know how to break the news. Finally, a couple of days into the rehearsal, she told Goldie.

"I hadn't had a girlfriend in so long that Goldie was the first one I told I was pregnant. When I told her, she cried silly! She told me to have lots of children and how much fun it was to be pregnant."

Goldie also remembered the moment. "I told her having children would be the most important, beautiful thing that would ever happen to her."

Liza's confiding in Goldie added an extra touch of closeness to their working relationship. Those on the set marveled at the rapport between the two stars, when not working, they would be found in their dressing room, laughing and gossiping like schoolgirls. The celebrity was stripped away, and the real person was shining through. It was a rare glimpse of Goldie.

Goldie and Liza Together aired on February 19, 1980. Unfortunately, its competition that night turned out to be coverage of the Winter Olympics, which cut into the show's ratings. Reviews were mixed: the show was considered nice but nothing spectacular.

Dusted off and once again set before Hawn was the script for *Best Friends*. She was still interested, which pleased director Norman

Jewison to no end. "I really loved Goldie," the director said, "and when I heard she was interested, I took a couple of meetings with her, and we agreed to do it as soon as she finished *Private Benjamin*."

The only missing part of the *Best Friends* equation was the male lead opposite Goldie. It would not be an easy role to cast. The actor had to have an obvious masculinity about him, but he also had to be able to project a believable sense of vulnerability. It also would not hurt if he was funny. Hawn immediately thought of Burt Reynolds. Goldie and the ruggedly handsome, macho actor had crossed paths over the years and had expressed a desire to work together.

"Goldie and I spent five years talking about making a movie together," said Reynolds. "We'd meet for dinner every once in a while and compare notes on scripts we had read. But we would always run up against the same problem—that one character always seemed to dominate the other. We couldn't find a script where there was give-and-take."

Reynolds had recently left his *Smokey and the Bandit* image behind and had been drawing praise for his work in more mature dramatic comedies. Consequently, Hawn's insistence on Reynolds was not met with the expected skepticism, and a script was messengered to the actor's home. As it turned out, Reynolds was thrilled with both the script and the prospect of finally working with Hawn.

Goldie's fondness for *Private Benjamin*'s comic possibilities only grew as the script took shape. In her eyes, the characters were believable, which accentuated the comedy. The physical shtick was breaking her up, and so she could only imagine what it would be like to actually get out in front of the camera and play army. She also began to see the realism behind the laughs and a bit of her own life reflected in the material.

"*Private Benjamin* points up some very tough, hard-edged realities," she explained. "My character is an Everywoman. She's been taught to be protected, spoiled, and taken care of. She's missed the revolution. She's the real unmarried woman, not the woman who walks away happy and in love. She walks alone but strong."

Hawn was showing a particularly strong business acumen as she put the various elements of *Private Benjamin* together. She formed separate companies for her production and acting duties and eliminated a large part of her tax burden by having her fees paid directly into those two accounts. Her production sense belied her rookie status as she negotiated the dollars-and-cents side of filming in Paris locations with a no-nonsense style. In Howard Zieff she had selected a director well versed in comic timing who could also be counted on to get across the more serious elements of the script.

Word of mouth and Hawn's emerging reputation resulted in the casting of such top-flight actors as Eileen Brennan, Armand Assante, and Harry Dean Stanton. Having endured the indignities of countless casting sessions over the years, Goldie was proving adept at selecting actors for even the most peripheral of roles.

Typical of the process was the number of handsome actors who paraded before the producer, vying for the role of Goldie's husband in the film. European actor Yves Renier had sharp features and piercing eyes. His good looks were not lost on Goldie. Though the producer in her ultimately felt he was not right for the part, Goldie the woman filed the memory of him away, thinking thoughts that only an unattached woman should think.

She was never what would be considered a method actor, but the element of *Private Benjamin* which required her character to go through basic training was something that Goldie felt had to be believable. So Hawn, with the cooperation of the U.S. Army, went through six weeks of basic training in late 1979 and early 1980 at Fort MacArthur, California, face-to-face with a screaming army drill sergeant. "After going through basic training, I would not resist the draft," the actress said after completing the rough-and-tough preparation. "Provided, of course, I could have a stunt double at all times."

Her growing confidence as an actress was boosted when *Foul Play* was released to rave reviews. Critics praised the chemistry between Chevy Chase and Hawn and pointed out that her return to the screen had resulted in a renewed sense of purpose. Up to her eyeballs in all things *Private Benjamin,* Goldie was happy but decidedly low-key about the success of *Foul Play.* "Nobody knows why these things happen," she offered. "You make your flops and you make your good stuff. If you survive all the bad stuff, then you have a fighting chance."

Quite the workaholic at this point, Hawn decided to take on yet another acting role when she was offered the chance to reunite with Chevy Chase in the Neil Simon comedy *Seems Like Old Times*. The film, a throwback to the screwball comedies of the 1940s, would feature Hawn as a successful lawyer whose ideal life with her second husband is disrupted when her first husband comes back into her life, seeking help when a couple of gangsters force him to rob a bank.

She agreed to do *Seems Like Old Times* right after completing *Private Benjamin*. Her decision to pile even more on an already full plate indicated how deep was her renewed commitment to her career. But more than one columnist was willing to go on the gossip superhighway with the story that Goldie was loading up on work in an attempt to avoid her increasingly uncomfortable relationship with Hudson. It did, in fact, appear that Hawn, despite her continued protests, was spending less and less time around the house, and that when she was around, her full attention was on Oliver and Kate. Hudson was becoming more and more of an afterthought.

Hudson's unhappiness with the turns his marriage was taking were becoming painfully evident. "I never had a sense of balance of marriage and work in my marriage to Goldie," Hudson said in looking back on those turbulent times.

Goldie threw herself into the dual role of producer-actor as *Private Benjamin* finally went before the cameras during the early months of 1980. It was on-the-job training of the toughest kind. Hawn would constantly have to shift mental gears from producer, counting every dollar spent and worrying about every minute of the schedule, to star, doing her best to wring the best possible performance out of every scene.

Typical of the way Goldie wore two hats were the frequent on-set conferences with director Zieff. One moment, she would be discussing the best way to play an upcoming scene. The next, she would be going over script pages, reminding the director that they needed to get a certain number of shots done that day to remain on schedule.

93

Crew members arriving at 7:00 A.M. would typically find Goldie already there, checking call times, attending to technical and financial concerns and fielding phone calls from Warner Bros. executives, who needed to know how things were going. Long after a day of filming ended, she would linger to view dailies and attend advertising and promotion meetings.

"Nobody wanted to hear Goldie say, 'We're due in Paris on Saturday, and so we must get this shot tonight,'" she said of her maiden voyage as producer. "And that meant I would have to tell them that we'd have to work until ten-thirty. But I took positions like that when it was necessary. In a few minutes, they'd have the set lighted and would be ready to do a take. Then I'd have to strip away the executive part of me instantly and go before the cameras as the actress to serve the needs of the scene and the director. It was an interesting thing to do, to discover how to maintain the balance."

According to Zieff, Hawn was on top of her game when it came time to drop the producer's hat and step in front of the camera. "You don't have to work hard with people like Goldie around. When I would talk about the concept of a scene, she would already be ahead of me."

Zieff was not alone in giving Hawn high marks for her demeanor and sense of style during the hectic shooting schedule. "She's a very smart woman," said costar Armand Assante. "She had a particular point of view about every scene she was involved in. I never had the sense that what we were doing was work. It always seemed like play. What she may have been going through internally is another thing. But she managed to keep a real positive bubble in the atmosphere."

During those hectic times, Goldie bent over backward to make sure her children did not miss her. Oliver, approaching age four, and Kate, a gurgling one-year-old, would come to the set on a regular basis and have lunch with Goldie in her trailer. "At night I'd run stoplights to get home in time to bathe them or just see them fall asleep. The movie was a big strain on me. I was being a mother, a wife, an actress, and a producer. But I still shut off the phones on the weekend and devoted my entire time to my family."

But while the bond with her children had remained strong, the relationship between Goldie and Hudson had become increasingly strained. They were communicating in a superficial manner, and the schedule Goldie was keeping was not affording them the kind of quiet time the couple obviously needed to sort things out. If Goldie was concerned, she wasn't showing it, and Hudson was uncharacteristically withdrawn and uncommunicative. Consequently, the problems in their marriage were allowed to fester, bringing emotional emptiness to both of them.

That summer *Private Benjamin* completed the U.S. portion of its schedule and moved the production to Paris for the final sequences. While in Paris, Goldie reportedly ran into Yves Renier. What she was feeling was most un-Goldie-like. She knew her husband was experiencing the panic of seeing his career going down the tubes and the growing inequality in their marriage. And yet she was very tempted by this handsome man and his attentions toward her. The kind, considerate, and sensitive side lost out to a Goldie who was suddenly feeling selfish and needy.

What happened next is open to conjecture. Some reports from that time indicate that the actress, sensing that her marriage to Hudson was in trouble and feeling the pangs of loneliness, fell into an immediate physical love affair with the French actor. Other reports indicated that the couple dated a few times but that a full-blown romance did not develop until much later. What was certain was that by the time the Paris portion of *Private Benjamin* had been completed, the pair had been spotted together on several occasions, and the gossip columns and tabloids were running wild with the story of Goldie's new love. For Bill Hudson, those stories were the straw that broke the camel's back.

Private Benjamin wrapped principal photography in August, but Goldie knew that a crazy work schedule still lay ahead in Los Angeles. She would be jumping right into *Seems Like Old Times* while simultaneously dealing with the massive postproduction editing designed to get *Private Benjamin* into theaters by October. She was looking forward to spending more time with her children, and according to interviews she gave during the latter stages of filming on *Private Benjamin*, she was also looking forward to spending more time with Bill.

Hawn was barely back on American soil when she was informed that Bill Hudson had filed for divorce on August 15.

"It was the most painful thing I've ever gone through," she recalled when she got the news. "This marriage was my dream. It was all I ever wanted. But people change. You mate, the person you love starts to change, and something happens to the relationship."

What happened in the aftermath of Hudson's filing for divorce, according to Bill's brother, Mark, was quick and quiet. "They didn't make any kind of formal declaration to the family. They didn't discuss it with us. They just stopped living together." Hudson moved out of the Pacific Palisades home and into the couple's Malibu residence.

Bill denied the rumors and bitter accusations and in particular the story that a relationship between Hawn and Chevy Chase that had started during the filming of *Foul Play* and was continuing on the set of *Seems Like Old Times* was integral to the breakup. "Nothing bad is going on between Goldie and me," he announced. "There will be no bitterly contested divorce or custody fight."

Hawn agreed that the divorce would not be a contentious one played out in the press and was grateful that Hudson had chosen to take the high road. But the shock of the divorce had admittedly left her scattered emotionally. "I don't know how I feel at this point. It's too new. I'm just trying to deal with the separation as well as I can right now."

Goldie had little time to feel sorry for herself, for she almost immediately found herself on the set of *Seems Like Old Times*, laughing it up over a hilarious Neil Simon script. "I howled all the way through when I read this script for the first time."

Simon, Chase, and director Jay Sandrich were well aware of Goldie's marriage problems and treated her with kid gloves, working around any perceived shifts in mood. Hawn, the consummate professional, was quickly able to block out the real world and concentrate on the work, for which she drew raves.

"She's a rare combination," said Simon. "She can be very funny and very sexy. She has a true appreciation of what's funny and what's bleak in life."

"Goldie has a good spirit," echoed her costar Charles Grodin. "She loves to laugh."

That Hawn was able to keep up her spirits was a miracle, for she was being pulled in four directions at the same time. Typical of her hectic life was the day on the *Seems Like Old Times* set when, after a long morning of shooting, Hawn used the first break of the day to rush off the set and into a conference with her *Private Benjamin* director and a Warner Bros. executive regarding some editing questions. Meeting completed, she returned to the set and was right in the middle of a complex dialogue scene when she realized she had neglected to get some information to her director in the just concluded meeting. Hawn yelled stop, called for a pencil and paper from an assistant, jotted down the items, and had the list sent immediately to the director before settling back into the scene, all without missing a beat.

Eileen Brennan, Hawn's costar in *Private Benjamin*, had moved easily into Goldie's circle of friends following the film's completion and had kept up with her current life through long telephone conversations. Brennan was amazed at the pace Goldie was keeping. "What Goldie did was incredible. She was filming *Seems Like Old Times*, attending meetings and signing memos on *Private Benjamin*, getting home in time to feed and play with the kids, and trying damned hard not to upset Bill. Her time was just being eaten up by commitments. She seemed to be taking it all in stride, but I knew she was going through some pain."

Hawn, physically and emotionally exhausted, completed *Seems Like Old Times* and saw *Private Benjamin* through the final phases of postproduction.

She once again retreated into an emotional cocoon. And despite feeling bad about leaving her children for a few weeks, Goldie decided once again to do what would be good for Goldie and took off for Africa alone. Rumors abounded that during that vacation she met up with Yves Renier in Europe and spent quite a bit of time with him. Whatever the truth of that vacation, one thing was certain: Goldie came back to the States very relaxed and reenergized.

Then the stresses inherent in dealing with divorce soon plunged her back into emotional turmoil.

During the months following Hudson's announced divorce plans, Goldie stayed pretty much at home, preparing her children, in subtle ways, for the fact that their dad would not be under the same roof and that she, at age thirty-five, was "gonna have to learn to date again." That comment, said only half in jest, was indicative of the positive spin she publicly put on the inevitable questions about the separation. And once again the press gave her an easy ride. The questions regarding her alleged liaisons with Renier and Chase and their implication in the breakup of her marriage were not asked, allowing her to come across as the innocent and the victim.

"The past is past," she acknowledged when the press came calling. "I don't dwell on the negatives in life. What's important is that I still have a beautiful future to look forward to."

But privately Goldie was shattered. Her hopes for a happily-ever-after life had once again crashed and burned. "If I ever had a life plan, I saw myself as happily married. I never saw myself as single with children and being frightened."

Nor had she ever believed that the discrepancy between Hudson's and her earning power would be a problem. "I really can't say how Bill felt about me earning the money. For God's sake! He was successful himself. But I guess it slowly dawned on me that he resented being second string."

In moments of bitterness Hawn was now openly doubting that a balance between her career and her personal life would ever be struck. Her father, always there with the right words at the right time in Goldie's life, told her that the bumps in her life should not come as a surprise. "He said, 'Goldie, you're an extraordinary woman who leads an extraordinary life. Your rules have to be different. Stop trying to apply the norm to yourself.'"

Goldie was only partially satisfied with her father's advice, holding stubbornly to the notion that she was really normal despite her stardom. "I do get far more recognition and publicity than most people. But that's my professional life. Other than that, what's so different about me?"

And then there were those moments when Goldie would throw aside any pretense of hope and wallow, occasionally on the record, in feelings of hopelessness. "A lot of dreams don't happen, and then you're confronted with real life. You learn life is not a storybook. It's tough to swallow...but you have to go on."

And going on for Goldie meant shielding her children as much as possible from the separation and the impending divorce. She would cook their meals, take Oliver to school, bathe them, and tuck them in at night.

"When I have to go off, it's much harder for me than it is for them," she said with a sigh. "It's hard to let go of your babies if they don't understand why you leave. It's important that they understand that I will come back. But when I call during the day, missing them terribly, they tell me not to worry, and I love that."

Her emotional state was buoyed by the response to *Private Benjamin*, which was released in the fall of 1980. Critics fell all over themselves praising the film, and especially Hawn, who received raves for an Oscar-caliber performance and for her considerable skills as a producer in simply getting the film made in the first place. The movie quickly made back its $10 million cost and was well on its way to grossing $50 million by Christmas.

It was during this period that Goldie made the acquaintance of a costume designer named Anthea Sylbert. As with most of her associations, it was initially a friendship based on the fact that, she laughingly recalled, "we both like to do lunch." But it quickly became evident that Hawn saw in Sylbert a kindred spirit. "We need each other's support. It gets lonely when you're out there doing a big job all alone. Most of us [women] in the industry were still pretty much underground, and we needed connections. We needed to exchange ideas and information."

For Sylbert, those meetings with Hawn were a happy surprise.

"When I met Goldie, the first thing I noticed was that she was much more sensible than I'd ever anticipated. She was not at all the ditzy person I had seen on-screen."

And what they discovered during those informal gabfests was that they had similar ideas about films—or as Goldie put it, "movies." "We agreed that *film* meant something esoteric and not necessarily something for everybody. When you're talking *movies,* you're talking something for the whole family."

Not too long after these meetings, Goldie took what would be considered the riskiest professional move of her career. With one producing credit on her resumé and the essentially untried Sylbert at her side, she formed Hawn/Sylbert Movie Company for the express purpose of making the kinds of movies they'd like to see.

Goldie's elation at the success of *Private Benjamin* and her first tentative steps in the direction of becoming a producing powerhouse would be short-lived. Because with the increased fame would also come terror.

Early in 1981, Goldie began getting crank telephone calls at all hours of the day and night. The first few times, she chalked up the calls to fan obsession and did not make too much of it. But as the calls continued, the unknown stalker's attentions began to play on her mind. She began to anticipate the worst every time the telephone rang.

She began taking the calls very seriously when the mystery caller began threatening her life. Visibly upset and concerned for the safety of her children and herself, Hawn went into a total panic when the caller escalated his reign of terror by having bouquets of red roses delivered to her front door. Goldie hired a bodyguard. Shortly after the bodyguard entered the picture, the roses stopped coming and the telephone calls became less frequent.

Even after the calls stopped for good, Goldie kept the bodyguard around for weeks more. Friends could see the emotional strain on her face. In a sad sort of way, celebrity had once again intruded on her private space and had taken just a bit more of her innocence away.

Meanwhile, Hawn started dating and was linked often but not

100

usually for long with any number of men. At one point, Tom Selleck was seen regularly on her arm. But she would inevitably find her way back into the arms, and the bed, of Yves Renier.

Hawn found much that drew her to this relationship with the attractive, romantic Frenchman. There was a daring and bravado in Renier that Goldie had not found in her previous lovers. And while nobody could get inside her head, the speculation was that Renier was serving as the one grand, no-strings-attached affair that she had never had because of her continual quest for love and stability.

That Goldie did not blink an eye when she discovered that Renier was, in fact, married spoke volumes about how seriously she was taking love and romance in her life. It seemed as if the prospect of yet another divorce had, at least temporarily, stripped away Goldie's long-held values regarding true love. She was deliberately avoiding the good men who might lead to love and a happy ending and instead kept falling into empty relationships that held no real future. Goldie was confused, scared, and attempting to find her way.

Ruth Buzzi, her longtime friend since the *Laugh-In* days, was convinced that Goldie's dating pattern and the superficial nature of the relationships was a smoke screen. "She may be going out with men, but the truth is, I feel she is really in need of a serious relationship."

Even her insightful mother, Laura Hawn, on the sidelines as Goldie's personal life was played out in the press, had her own insights into her daughter's behavior. "Goldie just isn't happy without a man to love her," she said. "But I'd like to see her with somebody who is not so competitive with her."

As with all things, Goldie was evenhanded about her personal life. She did not deny that she was dating around and keeping particular company with Renier. But she seemed nonchalant about the question of love and was candid about the fact that her growing power in the movie industry was still getting in the way.

"I'm in a kind of powerful position in the industry, and so it's a little difficult to find a man of equal achievement," she lamented. "But I'm not giving up. And the reason I'm not giving up is that I'm just a hopeless romantic."

These were the sentiments regularly expressed during family visits. Goldie and sister Patti became particularly close during this period. Her older sister was also experiencing a run of difficult relationships, and the two would regularly bemoan the fact that, according to Patti, "there would always be men coming in and out of our lives." Laura Hawn, in assessing her daughter's continuing relationship problems, stated, "It's very difficult for her to date. Men are intimidated by her."

Though she was keeping a lower profile, Hawn continued to work. She began to field all kinds of offers the moment *Seems Like Old Times* was in the can. She once again stepped back into television in the special called *Goldie Hawn in Paris*. The song-and-dance variety show, shot entirely on location at Paris's famed Moulin Rouge, allowed her an escape from the turbulence in her personal life and the opportunity to spend relatively uninterrupted time with Renier.

In the meantime, as the divorce was drawing to its conclusion, Hudson began getting cold feet about the end of his relationship with Hawn. "I still love her. Being married to Goldie was the best thing that ever happened to me. I'm just now beginning to realize what I've lost. She's truly a good friend and a wonderful human being. A man couldn't wish for a better mother for his children. I'd like to work things out. I think we still have a lot of love going for us."

He was candid in saying that their four-year-long marriage had succumbed to professional pressures. "It's difficult when you're both working hard at your careers. You finish up juggling emotions and time schedules, and in our case it just got out of hand."

Goldie was also having trouble dealing with the finality of her second divorce. While she believed her problems with Hudson were irreconcilable, she had to admit that he had been a wonderful father to their children. She would readily agree to Hudson's requests to see the children and would tell friends like Ruth Buzzi that "he's a terrific dad."

"After my divorce, I remember writing in my diary that I would never find another man who would love my children the way that I

102

do," she said. "That's why the divorce from Bill is so painful." But she felt that their marriage had passed the point of any possibility of reconciliation.

"You work hard in a marriage," she said when questioned about her feelings on the breakup of her second marriage. "You try to build it when you feel like it's breaking down. You try, and you don't stop. You don't throw it out at the first sign of trouble. So when you finally come to the realization that it's not going to work, you've earned the divorce. There are simply no questions."

The relationship with Renier continued to be regular tabloid fodder. Stories began circulating that Hawn had begun her affair with the French actor while shooting *Private Benjamin* and that it was her infidelity, not Hudson's insecurities or the implied relationship with Chevy Chase, that led to her husband's filing for divorce. In response to the reports, Goldie replied rather indignantly that she "would have gotten a divorce, anyway." There were also reports that Renier, during his relationship with Hawn, had not only returned to his wife on several occasions but had openly been flaunting his involvement with other women.

How much of these stories was true and how much was fabrication is open to interpretation. But with unsavory reports of her personal life becoming regular news, Goldie simply shrugged her shoulders.

"What can I say? Right now my personal life is all messed up. But I'm doing my best, taking it one day at a time."

In the meantime, *Seems Like Old Times* opened in theaters in January 1981 to mixed reviews and only fair box office. Typically, Hawn took the mixed response to the film in stride. There were rumors that Goldie, fresh off the success of producing *Private Benjamin,* had had some difficulty on the set of *Seems Like Old Times* simply being an actress after so recently having been in a decision-making role. She would only go as far as to say that there was a world of difference between acting and producing.

Goldie was once again beginning to feel her oats in regard to breaking out of the mold of comic actress. When she heard that a dramatic film adaptation of William Styron's novel *Sophie's Choice* was going to the screen, she moved heaven and earth to audition for the part of Sophie Zawistowska, the beautiful concentration-camp survivor whose intense relationships form the heart and soul of the story.

She really wanted the role and by all accounts gave a stirring audition. Unfortunately for her, Meryl Streep gave an even stronger one, and truth be told, her dramatic background made her less of a risk in this already risky project.

Hawn kept a relatively low profile through the remainder of 1981. She spent a lot of time with her children and her parents, whose visits to Los Angeles had become more frequent and longer in duration. Being around them was becoming increasingly important, as the health of her seventy-two-year-old father had begun to deteriorate. The sense of family was now uppermost in her mind. But so was her need to work, and just before Christmas, Goldie agreed to start work on *Best Friends* right after the first of the year.

In the meantime, Goldie had managed to sandwich in another television special. *Goldie and Kids...Listen to Us* was a radical departure from the lighter-than-air singing-and-dancing specials she had done in the past. Mixing in a few song-and-dance numbers, Goldie sat and talked and, most importantly, listened as young children talked frankly about their hopes and fears and about their attitudes toward sex, drugs, and the other issues children growing up in the 1980s faced. The show would ultimately receive rave reviews and moderate ratings when it aired in May 1981.

In January 1982, just before she was to report to the set of *Best Friends,* Hawn's father was admitted to the intensive care unit of Los Angeles's Cedar-Sinai Hospital, suffering the effects of a lifetime of smoking. It was with a heavy heart and mixed emotions that Goldie reported to the set of a film that was going to require her to be funny.

Director Norman Jewison saw other potential creative stumbling blocks in making *Best Friends.* For the film to work the characters had to be fabulously and believably in love. Even though actors have been faking that state since the birth of films, Jewison was concerned about the fact that Goldie was investing all her

104

romantic energy in Renier, while Reynolds was heavily involved with Loni Anderson. Two weeks before production began on *Best Friends,* the director suggested an unusual wrinkle in method acting.

"I suggested that Burt and Goldie go on a date," said Jewison. "I wanted them to become real pals in the playful sense that they would play in the film." Goldie and Burt were amused and willingly went along with the idea. During the course of the evening, the two costars talked about things personal as well as professional and so cemented the element of friendship that would, it was hoped, anchor *Best Friends.*

Best Friends turned out to be a trial for Goldie. She was once again faced with not being in on the decision-making process but remained less argumentative owing to the distractions of her father's illness. She settled into a strained routine. Days were spent attempting to generate laughs. At night, Goldie would rush to the hospital and her father's bedside, where she would often spend the entire night before going back to the set the following morning.

Goldie would later reveal that the nights spent at her father's bedside were a cathartic episode in her life. She would hearken back to her days as a child when she would bend over backward "to please him" and would finally deal with the fact that "there were never a lot of false compliments from Dad."

And now, during long nights in which she passed the time with her father with small talk or by reading his notes when he was too weak to respond, Goldie, at the final hour, was making peace with her father and herself. "The notes and the talking, maybe it was for selfish reasons," she recalled. "I wanted to let him know how important he had been in my life. I remember, one night, writing him a note while he was sleeping. I didn't want to wake him. The note read: 'You may have thought all your wisdom went in one ear and out the other, but it didn't.'"

During these trying times, Warren Beatty emerged as a rock. He would regularly accompany Hawn to the hospital and would often stay with her. Beatty was the first to notice that Goldie's physical condition was deteriorating along with her emotional state. She was barely eating, and sleep was a luxury she felt she could not afford.

105

Beatty recalled that on several occasions he would literally have to drag his friend away from her father's bedside and to the hospital cafeteria, where he would force a cup of soup into her.

Laura Hawn, no less upset by her husband's illness, remembered that her daughter "was very depressed." The depression stemmed, in part, from the fact that she was at her father's bedside on several occasions when he would suddenly take a turn for the worse. Goldie would race to the telephone and call the rest of the family. "I would say, 'This is it. Come to the hospital right away.'" Invariably, her father would pull out of it, sending Goldie's emotions into yet another tailspin.

Edward Rutledge Hawn died on June 7, 1982. For Hawn, the death of her father was the culmination of what she perceived, in her private thoughts, as the death of her pursuit of the American dream. Two divorces had resulted in her being the single mother of two children. Her most recent relationships with men had been scattershot affairs doomed to inevitable failure, and she, in all candor, was not seeing any real future with Yves Renier. Yes, she was a star of massive proportions. But her father was dead, and in her mind, so was a big part of her soul.

"Daddy made me a hard driver," she reflected not long after her father's death. "He taught me to be a realist. Because of Dad I never look at what I've got but what I don't know, what I haven't done and how I can do it. Dad taught me to be complete and to ask myself at night, Did I give enough quality time to my children? Did I make the right phone calls to advance my next project? And did I take enough time to go outside and look at my rosebushes?' My dad taught me that balance."

The synagogue was filled to capacity a few days later as family and well-wishers from the personal and professional sides of Goldie's life gathered to say goodbye to Edward Hawn. There were the expected prayers of mourning in preparation for the rabbi's taking the pulpit and giving the final eulogy. But moments before he was to step forward, the rabbi was told that his words would not be necessary.

Because Goldie Hawn would deliver the eulogy, even though she was not quite sure what she was going to say.

There was an audible murmur in the synagogue as she made her way to the pulpit. Goldie smiled, a tight, nervous smile. The eulogy began in an uncharacteristically somber tone as Goldie proclaimed her father "a king among kings" and went on in that reverential tone for several minutes. Then something in her head clicked. This was not the way her father would have wanted his eulogy to be. He would want it light and funny.

And so, as the eulogy continued, Hawn's humor slowly began to take over. First snickers and finally full-blown guffaws greeted her tales of her father's life and the advice he had given her. The mood shifted to a tearful but joyous tribute that, in Goldie's spirited delivery, celebrated the life of Edward Rutledge Hawn in a way that only a loving daughter could. As she left the pulpit and filed out of the synagogue, Goldie, for the moment, felt at peace with her father's passing.

But she could not be expected to totally leave the sadness behind, and so Goldie found the remainder of the filming of *Best Friends* an emotional ordeal. But one that she came through with flying colors, according to costar Reynolds. The actor recalled that in between takes Goldie would often be found in her trailer, sobbing. "But whenever director Jewison needed her, she wiped away her tears, would come out on the set, and would just nail her lines with impeccable timing and humor," Reynolds said. "Anyone else would have folded. Given the strain she was under with the death of her father, she defined the word professional."

And when she could block out the pain, Goldie found truly creative moments. The script for *Best Friends* was well written, but Jewison saw the opportunities for improvisation, and in Hawn and Reynolds he had two actors who were more than willing to play. Some of what Goldie considered the best moments in the film, including a wonderful pantomime sequence, were the result of on-the-spot play.

"She brought out a gentleness in Reynolds that I don't think we've ever seen before," said Jewison.

With the completion of *Best Friends*, Hawn returned to the life of a single mother and the final stages of her divorce from Hudson.

The decree, unlike that of her first marriage, was rather amicable. Hudson would get possession of the couple's Malibu home. With Hudson working, no alimony on either side was asked for or granted. Hudson would have joint custody of the children, which was the way Goldie wanted it.

Hawn insisted that her mother leave Takoma Park and move to Los Angeles. She agreed and was soon living in a condo not far from Goldie's Pacific Palisades home. Things seemed to be slowly but surely getting back to normal as Goldie closed in on her thirty-seventh birthday.

Then, only four months after the death of her father, Goldie watched in horror as her good friend Eileen Brennan was hit by a speeding car.

9

First Comes Guilt...
Then Comes Love

EILEEN BRENNAN'S ACCIDENT WAS GOLDIE HAWN'S FAULT. AT least that's the way Goldie saw it.

Hawn and Brennan had become good friends on the set of *Private Benjamin*. When the film spun off into a weekly television series, she was thrilled when Brennan was signed to reprise her role as a tough military woman. Partially to celebrate her friend's success and more likely as an excuse to get together and dish, Hawn arranged for the pair to meet at a Venice, California, restaurant for an early dinner on the evening of October 27, 1982.

As often happens in Hollywood, Goldie was running late and so debated whether to cancel her dinner with Brennan or just show up, hoping the actress had decided to wait. Goldie finally arrived an hour and a half late and was happy to find that her good friend had been patient.

The pair spent the early hours of the evening lingering over espresso, chatting and laughing about their families, the business, talking about everything and nothing. Goldie was enjoying one of those rare evenings when she could loosen up and relax. The two were still laughing and giggling as they walked outside the restaurant after dinner and prepared to depart.

Brennan started across the street and turned to wave goodbye to Goldie. At that moment a car came speeding out of the darkness and struck her with a sickening thud. Brennan was hurled up and then landed on the car's windshield. The speeder continued another seventy feet down the street before screeching to a halt, causing Brennan to fall into the street. Goldie ran to her friend in hysterics, screaming and crying as she bent over her body. Brennan was barely conscious as Goldie took her in her arms. Her body was twisted in frightening directions. Blood was streaming from her face, head, and legs.

"Goldie saw the whole accident coming," recalled Laura Hawn of the conversations she had with her daughter after the accident. "But she said she was just too paralyzed to call out."

Goldie stayed with Brennan while a restaurant employee called an ambulance. She only moved a few feet away when the ambulance arrived and the attendants began to work on her friend. The expressions on their faces told her that it did not look good. Hawn followed the ambulance carrying Brennan to the hospital that night and, in a scenario reminiscent of the vigil at her father's bedside, stayed with Brennan until morning.

The initial prognosis was not good. She had suffered crushed legs, a fractured skull, and crushed bones in her face. Eileen Brennan might not live through the night. Hawn got on the phone and called Brennan's two sons, her sisters, and her ex-husband. She did not want them to get the news from anybody but her.

As the night wore on, Goldie was running on adrenaline and nothing more. She was frightened, concerned, and most of all, guilty.

"Goldie carried a lot of guilt over that accident," her mother recounted. "She wished she had canceled the date in the first place and wondered whether fate would have been kinder if she had not been late."

After being assured by doctors that there was nothing she could do, Goldie finally left the hospital at five A.M. She drove home in a daze, tears streaming down her face. It was as if the accident had finally brought all the pain and anguish of the past couple of years to the surface. Goldie pulled into the driveway of her Pacific Palisades home just as the sun was coming up. She went into the house, opened the door to her room, closed the door behind her, climbed into bed, and broke down sobbing.

She would not get out of bed for two days.

"I have seen Goldie go through a lot," her mother remembered. "I've seen her divorces. I've seen her defeats. But I had never seen her unable to get out of bed before."

Brennan miraculously survived but was in a delicate state when she returned home after about a month. Goldie was at Brennan's house on a regular basis for a number of months, attending to her every need. In Goldie's heart, she felt she was paying penance—Not only for her friend's accident but for all the failures in her life that had finally caught up with her.

Goldie struggled through the next few months in the bluest of funks. Her personal life was in shambles, and her professional feelings were also hurt when *Best Friends* was released in December 1982 to mediocre reviews and box office. Hawn did little in the way of a postmortem, saying only that she had not been the producer on that film and that if she had been she would have made different choices.

Personally, Goldie's life continued in turmoil. Yves Renier was still around and occupying her entire romantic life. But she was seeing him less often, and the consensus among friends and gossip columnists was that the relationship was beginning to cool.

At this time, Goldie rarely discussed Renier even with her closest friends, which was par for the course, for when it came to her personal thoughts, she was admittedly scattered. "I've thought about moving up to Oregon for a few years. But I'm a single woman, and I don't want to lock myself up in a cabin. And I don't think I'm ready to hook up with a lumberjack.

"But being single isn't so bad." Hawn chuckled, finding mild amusement even in her depressed moments. "You might say going to bed with an Oscar isn't much fun, but at least it's peaceful."

One thing was certain: Goldie, who continued to fluctuate between blaming herself and her husbands for her divorces, would think long and hard before she ever considered marriage again. "Before marrying any man, I'd have to know him pretty well," she said. "I'd have to know the inside of his head."

While the question of relationships weighed heavily on her following the completion of *Best Friends*, she cried often and admitted that much of her confusion and guilt was the result of her father's death. "I'm really not over it. I don't think I'll ever be able to get over it."

The lone bright spot in her life continued to be family. With her sister, Patti, and Patti's two teenage sons now living in Los Angeles, adding to the circle occupied by Oliver, Kate, and her mother, the Hawn clan spent all their free time together. When Patti's son David appeared in a high school play, Goldie and the rest of the family showed up with video cameras to record the event. The first Christmas without Goldie's father was the expected solemn event, but the family brightened up at year's end with a trip to the trendy vacation town of Sundance, Colorado.

After a week of frolicking in the snow and tobogganing, the Hawn family went over to Barbra Streisand's house to ring in 1983. Goldie's smiling, laughing face as the clock struck midnight was an indication that the guilt and anguish were leaving her and that life, like the new year, was about to begin again.

The expected pile of scripts was awaiting Goldie's perusal in the new year. Some were lousy; others were interesting and showed potential. However, still stinging from the frustrations she experienced with *Seems Like Old Times* and *Best Friends*, Goldie was not looking to get into another situation in which somebody else would be calling the shots. It was at that point that she fell in love with a script called *Swing Shift*.

Swing Shift told the straightforward tale of a woman who starts work in an aircraft plant during World War II, after her husband goes off to war, and subsequently falls in love with another man. She loved the simplicity of the story but saw much more in the way of possibilities for the film.

"I thought the movie should feel like a musical," she said. "The costumes, the attitude, and the love affairs all had to have a real element of sexuality about them. It had to capture that sorority feeling that happened during the war when men went away and women took over the workforce."

Not wishing to trust this project to other hands, Goldie immediately attached herself as executive producer and, based on the success of *Private Benjamin,* felt she would have no trouble setting up a deal for the film with a major studio. She figured wrong. "Even with my newfound credibility, *Swing Shift* was a very hard sell," she said with a sigh. "It wasn't another Goldie-joins-the-army movie. It was a period piece, and so the sets and costumes would be very expensive."

Goldie had calculated that *Swing Shift* could be made for $14 million, a lot of money in 1983. Even those studios willing to make the movie with Hawn as producer were reluctant to spend that kind of money, but Goldie, who had learned the art of wheeling and dealing during the trial by fire that was *Private Benjamin,* patiently weighed in with the facts.

"This time I said, 'Look, you guys are money people. You can't always envision how a script will look on the screen. I'm here as a creative person to enlighten you about what *Swing Shift* can be so at least you'll know what you're turning down."

She hit many logical and convincing high points in those meetings. There was the fact that "*Swing Shift* was a war movie about the people who were left behind." She was passionate in painting the picture of the "women who went into the factories and cooked and brought home the paychecks." And she was often near tears as she battered the bean counters with thoughts of "the love affairs that developed when you never knew if you were going to see your husband again."

But the studios continued to pass on *Swing Shift.* Warner Bros., playing hardball, finally put an offer on the table. "They said, 'We'll give you half, and you find the other half,'" Hawn recounted, still angry at the memory of the offer. "I said, 'No, damn it! I'm not going to show up half the time for work.'"

Warner Bros., feeling the heat of Hawn as a power player they did not want to get on the wrong side of, eventually kicked in the entire budget on *Swing Shift*. The next step was to find a director who would have the slightly out of kilter approach to filmmaking that would serve the mystical, timeless qualities of her film. That director turned out to be newcomer Jonathan Demme.

Demme had come to Hawn's attention on the strength of a reputation for energetic exploitation films like *Caged Heat* and *Crazy Mama* and the critically acclaimed bio picture *Melvin and Howard*. "I thought Demme was just the guy who could bridge the forties and the eighties," she recalled after her initial meeting with the director. "He walked into my office one day and looked adorable, very hip, dressed absolutely right. He said, 'I can do this picture. I know what it's about.'"

The young director was saying exactly the things Goldie wanted to hear. "I see *Swing Shift* as a strong relationship comedy. This movie won't be another screwball comedy."

Goldie was sold. "I saw great talent there, and so I called the studio and said 'I love this guy!' Everybody said great, and we made a deal."

Demme, a tightly wound, somewhat closed personality, laughed off the warnings he had been given that he was entering a potentially problematic situation with Hawn. "I'd been warned from the start that I might run into problems on *Swing Shift*. But I love actors, and so I always believed it was possible to work things out."

After selecting Demme to direct, casting the role of her film lover, Lucky, was the toughest element of the film. There had to be a touch of arrogance mixed with decency and the slightest bit of vulnerability and whimsy in her 4-F love interest. She knew that would be a tall order for even the most accomplished actor. Goldie saw a lot of actors for the role and at one point was even seriously considering Demme's suggestion that rock-and-roller Bruce Springsteen would be perfect for the part.

Until Kurt Russell walked back into her life.

Russell, thirty-five, had grown in the ensuing years from a cute, gangly teen into a ruggedly handsome man with sparkling eyes and an impish grin. In Hollywood circles Russell had come to be known as a reliable B-level actor. He was on time, believable, especially in action films, and had a laid-back, easygoing charm that made him a favorite among producers, directors, and casting people. Russell and director John Carpenter had formed a particularly strong tie, with the actor appearing in Carpenter's *Escape From New York* (1981) and *The Thing* (1982). It was with Carpenter's television biography of Elvis Presley that Russell, in the hip-shaking title role, began to turn heads.

While filming the Presley bio, Russell met and married his costar, Season Hubley. The marriage was an emotional roller coaster that lasted four years and produced one child. At the height of his popularity, Russell willingly took a year off from acting to stay home with his son while his wife attempted to reestablish her career. When the marriage finally ended, he was wracked with guilt, taking much of the blame for the breakup and feeling immense pain for what the divorce would do to his son. What followed for Russell was a seemingly endless string of meaningless relationships that left the actor feeling detached from the concept of a normal family life. "I had begun to feel that my lot in life was not to feel that way with another person."

Consequently, he was all business when he read the script for *Swing Shift;* he was not impressed. "My feeling at the time was, Why would anybody want to go and see this picture? I've seen this picture at least a thousand times. But I was interested in working with Goldie, and so I went in."

The actor, always a man of a few words, recalled the casting session with a decided bit of understatement. "I walked in, and we met each other again. I said, 'Do you remember me?'"

She did, and instantly flashed back one year to the day she was in a movie theater with a friend watching the very grown up Russell in *The Thing,* when somebody in the row behind her exclaimed, 'Wow! What a hunk!' Goldie had to agree.

"When I met Kurt again, he felt like family," she recalled. "I felt extremely comfortable with him, and I was instantly attracted."

Hawn and Russell talked at length about the part. They started to get hungry and adjourned the conversation to a nearby restaurant, where they continued talking about the particulars of *Swing Shift.*

115

The chemistry beyond a business relationship already seemed to be bubbling through. They laughed easily, and their eyes rarely left each other. It was almost an afterthought that Russell seemed to have a handle on the character. Goldie finally got up to leave, and as she crossed the crowded restaurant, Russell yelled, "Even if I don't get the part, I'd love to take you out sometime."

Russell won the role of Lucky, and as the starting date for *Swing Shift* drew closer, neither he nor Hawn felt that the experience would be anything more than a good friendship to balance out their working days. Neither of them, on the surface, seemed ready for a relationship. Hawn was still gun-shy and spending all of her time with the still-married Renier, when she was with anybody at all, and the tensions that would inevitably arise surrounding her starring and producing *Swing Shift* hardly left time for even a hint of romance. And besides, Goldie was a firm believer in not mixing business with pleasure.

Russell, for his part, seemed equally unavailable. He was more concerned with being a good father to his son, Boston, than with starting another serious relationship but was seeing a handful of women at the time.

Unbeknownst to Hawn, her good feelings about director Demme were about to change. Once Warner Bros. had agreed to Demme's directing *Swing Shift,* they entered into separate negotiations with him. What Goldie would later discover was that Demme, according to Hawn, "wanted a lot of my powers as producer and star reduced."

When filming started, she was immediately aware of an adversarial relationship developing between her and Demme. The director, true to his word, was not making a star vehicle; he was paying a lot of attention to the film's period details and the supporting characters. The buzz on the set during those early days of filming was that Goldie was coming across as a highly paid extra. It was as if the director had suddenly lost interest in his star's character.

"I realized that certain things were wrong," Goldie remembered. "Even though we had a script in place, scenes were being written as we were filming. Also, we were shooting very little coverage, which is insane because a lot of movies are virtually made in the cutting room. And I discovered that Jonathan was very uneasy about working with a movie star."

While she was concerned with what was happening to her movie, Goldie was not pushing the issue, largely because her friendship with Russell was quickly turning into something more. At least one crew member had already speculated on how great it would be if the film duo became a couple in real life. Hawn realized, not too long after filming began, that romance was in the air. "When we started filming, I realized that my feelings for him went much deeper than friendship."

Russell and Hawn took the next big step one night after work. It had been a particularly exhausting day, and the inconsistencies of Demme's approach to making the film were continuing to be a distraction to Goldie. Russell and Hawn decided to go dancing at a local branch of the Playboy Club. When they were not up on the dance floor, they were deep in conversation. There was some shop talk. Russell listened patiently as Goldie poured out her feelings about Demme and the direction the picture was taking. But there was also a not too subtle undertone to the small talk and laughs. They were taking the tentative first steps in a mating dance.

"I'll be honest," said Russell, laughing, "I was first attracted to Goldie because she had a great behind. But I quickly discovered that she also had a great mind and that our senses of humor mixed well."

By the time their evening of dancing was over, Russell and Hawn were feeling a strong need to be alone. She was renovating her Pacific Palisades home and staying with the kids at her mother's Malibu Beach condo. Russell was staying with his brother-in-law.

"We had no place to go," recalled Russell of their dilemma. "So we decided to break into the house Goldie was having renovated. We walked around the house and eventually found our way to the master bedroom. I turned to Goldie and said, 'This is where the bed goes.' I remember looking at Goldie and thinking, Do I really want to do this? So we were on the floor of the master bedroom, and the next thing we knew, there were flashlights shinning in our eyes. A local security company had come to the house to check to see if there had been a break-in. We were lying there naked, and all of a sudden we just started laughing."

Later that evening, the couple checked into a nearby motel, where they made love for the first time. "I didn't want to leave her," recalled Russell of that first night of passion. "This girl was a crack-up. She was just like me."

Hawn, in the afterglow of their lovemaking, was also feeling euphoric. "It was wildfire," she said of their first night together. "I knew I really liked this guy. He was perfect."

"It happened real quick," said Hawn of their love. "I was real nervous because I didn't want it to be a fly-by-night deal. We spent that first evening together, and after he dropped me off at my mother's apartment, I remember the rest of the weekend being unbearable because I couldn't see him. It wasn't lust. I just wanted to hang out with him. And I thought, When I come in to work on Monday, it will really be fun because there will be no pretense about our relationship.'"

But it was during that weekend apart that Goldie realized that her liaison with Russell might in fact be nothing but the one-night-stand she feared.

He had been up-front about the fact that he couldn't see her that weekend because "he had a girlfriend coming to the set for a visit." Goldie had not told Kurt she was still carrying on a relationship with Renier and that he, too, was about to come to town for a visit. Over that weekend, Goldie made the decision to take a chance and follow her heart.

"I had to call and tell him [Renier] that I had fallen in love with somebody else. It was very hard because I had been dating this guy for four years. But I knew it had to be that way."

Goldie came to the set Monday, giddy at the prospect of being free and in love and apprehensive about what would happen when she ran into Kurt. She decided that the lighthearted approach was the best.

"I walked up to him and said, 'So how was it? Have fun?' Kurt said, 'She never showed up! She stood me up!' I was happy. I was thrilled."

The pair returned to work, determined to be discreet about the turn their relationship had taken. But they did a bad job of hiding it. Crew members would regularly see them walking hand in hand. Despite the continuing pressures of the shoot, they always seemed to be happy. And once, following a particularly hot-and-heavy love scene, Hawn laughingly said, "Honey! This is nothing like what goes on at home!"

Russell had also gotten into the spirit of the sparks that were flying between them. During a particularly hectic day on the set, he sidled up to her during a break in filming and said, "I can't wait until this picture is over so that we can really have some fun."

Her affair with Russell was helping to shield her from the minefield that making *Swing Shift* had become. Still clinging to her initial impressions of Demme, Goldie continued to relent on a number of fronts. She was content to fight her instincts and be the actress and not the producer. When the director approached her one day with the suggestion that she not watch dailies, she said, "Fine, if it makes you nervous."

"I was hoping it was going to be a smooth experience because I didn't want to have to deal with anything else," she confessed. "I didn't want Demme to think that he was working with a movie-star–tycoon, so I gave in and never saw any of the dailies. I also let a lot of things slip by that I normally would have discussed with a director, one who would be able to decipher the fact that I had a point of view and that I was no threat to him."

Adding to her growing list of problems on *Swing Shift* was the concern from the studio that the original budget was not going to be sufficient. Goldie fell into a panic mode, fighting to save every scene that was cut and every extra who was removed from a crowd sequence. Finally, in a last-ditch attempt to save the artistic integrity of the film, Hawn conceded the very thing she had fought so hard for in the first place.

"I kicked in my executive producer's money. I even gave away my producer's credit, [which put her producer's salary into the budget]. For me, the movie was a labor of love, and I was doing everything I could to save the film."

119

Swing Shift finally completed filming early in 1984. While Demme was ensconced in the editing room, Hawn remained true to her agreement with the director to stay away. In the meantime, she had much to occupy her time. She turned to motherhood with a vengeance, spending a great deal of quality time with her children.

With her producing partner, Anthea Sylbert, Goldie had finally found their first project under the Movie Company banner. It was called *Protocol,* and it was about a cocktail waitress who ends up working for the State Department after she inadvertently stops the assassination of a prominent Arab official. Comic misadventures ensue as she runs afoul of corrupt politicians and foreign intrigue en route to a finale in which she ends up running for Congress.

Sylbert would be handling the lion's share of the production chores, and with the always reliable Buck Henry scripting, *Protocol* would be the acting-only job she needed after the strain of producing *Swing Shift.* And, of course, there was Kurt.

Hawn and Russell were leery of on-set romances and, despite the passion they continued to have for each other, were inclined to take it slow after the completion of *Swing Shift.* Russell was scheduled to go to Italy almost immediately to star in the film *Ladyhawke,* while Goldie would begin preproduction on *Protocol.* They were uncomfortable with the idea of being apart, but Hawn, in the wake of her two well-publicized failed marriages, was direct in her final conversation with Russell before he left for Italy.

"You know, honey, we're up for grabs," she told him. "I'm going to be here, and I love you. But life doesn't stop. We just don't know if our romance will last."

Russell went off to Italy with a heavy heart and immediately began having creative and personal difficulties with the direction of the picture. "It was a big production. I had no confidence in myself and the idea of appearing in a costume. And I was away from Goldie and would be for five months."

Russell wanted to come home in the worst way, and it would not have taken much for him to quit. He was looking for some kind of sign. He called Goldie. "She was fantastic," he said of that conversation. "She pointed out that it would be five months on location and that I was on the other side of the world. I told her I was feeling bad and choked off."

Russell hung up the phone and after some final deliberation made the decision to risk a major blow to his career by quitting Ladyhawke and leaving the production in the lurch. In Russell's mind, love had conquered all. "I was surprised by the way I felt about Goldie and the way she looked. After meeting Goldie, I realized I could just be who I was and someone would take me for that and not hold it against me."

A week later, he was back in the States and letting himself into the hotel room Goldie was staying in during the renovation process. She was not there. Russell quickly scribbled a note, walked into the bedroom, and shut the door.

The note Goldie read when she finally got back said, 'Take your clothes off. I'm in the next room.'

"After the movie, we both just wondered what was going to happen," Russell reflected. "But the more time we spent with each other after the picture, the better and faster things seemed to go."

Hawn was not worried that getting involved with yet another show-business person was a blueprint for disaster. "I never really thought about it in those terms," she remarked when questioned about her choice of men. "I don't think I'd have much fun with someone who didn't really understand my business from a very deep level. The secret to making a show-business relationship work is to find someone who is not a weak person and who also understands the business. In Kurt I think I've got the best. I feel very lucky."

The luck continued when Goldie made what she considered the all-important decision to introduce Kurt to her children. Oliver and Kate, still confused in the aftermath of Goldie's split with Hudson, were a bit leery of this strange man, but Russell's personality and quite natural fatherly instincts soon won them over. In short order, Goldie was introduced to Russell's son, Boston. The young boy was likewise a bit shy at first, but Goldie's warmth eventually drew him out of his shell.

Unfortunately, her luck in regard to *Swing Shift* was about to turn very bad. Demme announced that he had finally completed the first cut of *Swing Shift,* and so, on a chosen day, Hawn and a handful of executives filed into a Warner Bros. screening room. There were smiles and good-natured small talk as everyone settled into their seats and the lights went down. There was stone silence when the lights came up. The executives were shifting uncomfortably in their seats, and Goldie was visibly upset. She made some quick goodbyes and rushed out of the screening room.

"After I saw that first cut of *Swing Shift,* I went to a friend's house, and when she came home, I was lying facedown on her front lawn, crying," she sadly recalled. "I was devastated! What I saw was not the movie I sold to Warner Bros."

She was not alone in her assessment that Demme had succeeded in sucking all the life and magic out of the film. Warner's studio executives, while less emotionally involved in the film than Goldie, were also in agreement that Demme had not delivered the film he had promised. But they also agreed that first cuts were just that and that there might still be a good movie somewhere within the soulless mess they had just seen.

A series of meetings with Demme ensued, some with the executives and some with Goldie. Hawn, who had stuck her neck out to get Demme on the film, was feeling caught in the middle. "I didn't want him fired at that point," she insisted. "I was the person who thought he could do it. He did not have a track record, but he was the darling of the critics, and so I went on instinct."

Her meetings with Demme were tense. She was passionate in what she liked and, more importantly, in what she did not like about the film. And what she did not like could fill volumes. The story, in Demme's hands, had become unfocused and forced. There was a matter-of-fact nature to the way the characters were drawn that failed to bring out their specialness. That Goldie's character was relegated largely to the background of the story was only part of the problem. That there was no central character the audience could identify with was a bigger one. Demme was equally adamant that what he had given Goldie were the very things they had agreed upon in preproduction meetings. But there was no screaming or ugliness.

122

He was quietly amenable to Goldie's suggestions and left those meetings armed with suggested changes that he assured the studio and star he would most certainly make.

"Jonathan would say yes to all our ideas," lamented Hawn. "Then he'd go away and come back and show us the movie again and there would be none of the things that we discussed in it. This went on for quite a while, and the studio didn't know what to do. Nobody was getting the results we wanted."

Writer-director Robert Towne, who was in the *Swing Shift* loop at the time, was candid in saying that part of the problem with the film was Hawn's unwillingness to assert the star power she had. "She was fearful of confronting Demme. She was letting him do what he wanted to do. She would suggest that 'this would be better.' He would say, 'Okay,' and then not do any of it. Goldie wouldn't argue about it."

To make matters worse, Demme had decided to make the *Swing Shift* problems public, going to the press with tales of how difficult Hawn had been during filming and how she was putting him through postproduction hell with her unreasonable demands. "It was a good experience until we got into postproduction," exploded the irate director. "All of a sudden, Warner Bros. and Hawn wished they had made a star vehicle instead of an ensemble piece."

He further intimated that Goldie was pulling the classic star trip and that when she did not get her way, she had threatened to go to the studio and get him fired. Goldie, who allowed that she did have some conversations with the Warner Bros. people but insised that she at no time threatened to fire Demme, was upset, to say the least.

"He went to the press and said some terrible things. His publicly hanging out all that wash was a terrible thing. Still, I held no malice toward him."

Not wanting to see *Swing Shift* go down the tubes, she finally did the very thing Demme had already accused her of doing. She went to the Warner Bros. studio heads and as tactfully as possible told them she did not think the film worked in its present form and that Demme was not capable of making an acceptable film with the footage that had already been shot. She then insisted it would be in everybody's best interest to hire another director to shoot additional footage that would fill in the film's holes.

Faced with the threat of replacement and realizing the damage it would do to his reputation in Hollywood, Demme reluctantly agreed to do the reshoots to Goldie's specifications. The studio agreed it was the only way to save the film, and so the actors once again convened on the studio lot, where some bridging scenes, written by Towne and designed to make sense of the confusing points of view and shaky characterization, were shot.

But once the reshoots began, Hawn discovered that Demme was going to push this war of wills to the bitter end. He immediately brought up the fact that Goldie had given up her producer's credit and so did not have approval rights on any of the reshoot footage. It also became obvious by his actions that the director was doing the reshoots under protest. "Jonathan just sat on the set while the cameras rolled," Goldie reported. "He was there, but he wouldn't have anything to do with the filming."

Demme, appeared totally bent on self-destruction when he insisted that he would not put any of the new footage into the final cut of the film. At this point, Goldie and Warner Bros. had had enough. The studio and Hawn stepped in, taking the director officially off the film and supervising its final editing themselves.

In looking back at the added footage, Hawn conceded that it was only a bandage. The new scenes tended to strengthen the female roles, and on the plus side, Christine Lahti's caricature of a working woman gained added substance. The male roles were given little help by the new footage, remaining flat, unsympathetic, and unfocused in their development. The editing process on yet another cut of *Swing Shift* continued. At this point, any enthusiasm for the film had dissipated. Goldie and the studio just wanted to get it behind them, and so *Swing Shift*, while not perfect, was eventually completed to everybody's satisfaction. Except Demme's.

"The film was mutilated," said the exasperated director. "They replaced a third of what had been shot and took a very fine film that had something important to say and turned it into a schizophrenic mishmash. It was a demoralizing experience."

Christine Lahti remained neutral in her memories. She remembered that she did have some disagreements with Hawn at the editing stage of the picture. "But there was no feud. She and I disagreed, perhaps, about the way the film was being edited, but overall I had a great experience."

And so finally *Swing Shift* was a hard-fought and bitter lesson for Hawn. She had seen a wonderful vision compromised. She had seen her position challenged and had, to a large degree, caved in. Nobody was satisfied with the compromises made on the film, least of all the folks at Warner Bros., who were culpable in the disaster. A stronger executive hand might have seen the troubles developing early on and replaced Demme. But Hawn had made the director her fair-haired boy, and Warner Bros. had not wanted to make their star unhappy. Bottom line, there was plenty of blame to go around.

On the professional front she had proved she could swim with the big fish. Though *Swing Shift* was a commercial failure, Goldie's getting the film off the ground despite studio indifference and her insistence on getting the film done no matter what it took showed the Hollywood community she had what it took to get movies made.

"Yeah I'm tough," she acknowledged following the *Swing Shift* debacle. "When I need to be there and do it...yeah, I'm tough. Which doesn't mean that I don't soften or cry, don't get upset and don't feel awful. But I just can't sit there and be victimized by everything."

10

Think Alike, Love Alike

GOLDIE AND KURT TRIED TO PROLONG THE INEVITABLE.

Business meetings and preproduction schedules were constantly being juggled. Their time together became more intense and passionate. For Hawn the days following the completion of *Swing Shift* were some of the happiest in her life. The couple and their children were splitting time between Goldie's Pacific Palisades home and Russell's Aspen, Colorado, digs. Russell painted an idyllic picture of their early days together.

"We'd work around the house, go to the movies once in a while, and spend time with friends. In the winter we'd ski, and I'd take the kids sledding. Goldie would have people from the studio over when she was getting ready to do *Protocol,* and she'd put on these great parties. Before I met Goldie, the only people I knew in the business were the people I had worked with. Now I was meeting all kinds of people."

Goldie, who made no bones about the fact that she was a city girl, was apprehensive about living even a small part of her life in the wilderness that was Kurt's world. Nevertheless, during those early visits to her lover's home, when Kurt showed Goldie a horse up close and led her gingerly around a grazing herd of cattle, she nervously speculated that she could get used to this. "Kurt is going to teach me to rope cattle," she said enthusiastically. "I have this vision of my getting on a horse and going out and rounding up cattle and it's great and the horse runs away with me and I get thrown and I wind up in a creek. And it all sounds so great!"

During this time the couple also had their first extended holiday together, spending time in Morocco, Spain, Paris and London. They took in the sights, made love often, and began establishing the signs and looks to communicate the way only commited lovers do. It was during the Morocco leg of their vacation that they discovered, firsthand, how bright Goldie's star shined.

They had been wandering the streets of a remote Moroccan village when they stopped into a small storefront to have their fortunes told by a tarot card reader. People walking by recognized Goldie and gathered around the storefront. The crowd grew larger and larger, and before they knew it, an estimated four hundred people were watching them. A bemused Russell remarked of the incident: "With Goldie, it's always a circus."

Neither Russell nor Hawn would go into too much detail about their travels other than to say they had a wonderful time. Russell, always the master of cryptic understatement, did offer: "I'm much better playing in life than working in it."

They eventually returned to the States, where their lives became further intertwined. At Goldie's insistence, Russell gave up smoking. The result was that in three weeks he put on eight pounds. Goldie's solution was to insist that Russell join her aerobics class. For a time Russell would dutifully stand in the back of the room, sweating off the pounds while the primarily female class spent their time craning their necks to look at him.

The couple's conversations also began to reflect their closeness. Phrases like "I said to Goldie" and "Goldie and I" began to pepper Russell's conversation. With Goldie there was a lot of "Kurt did this" and "You should have heard what Kurt said."

By mid-1984 reality set in, and both had commitments to film projects that could no longer be put off. And so it came to pass that Hawn was kissing Russell goodbye as he hopped a plane to Miami, Florida, to star in the film *Mean Season;* she remained in Los Angeles to film the first part of *Protocol.*

The days and weeks leading up to the separation had been a blur of incidents and emotions, many of them mundane, but all were, in terms of the couple's flowering relationship, important. There was time alone together and time with their children. The closer they grew, the more they seemed to discover about each other. And what they were finding out pleased them to no end.

"Kurt is the least competitive man I know," Goldie said not too long after their relationship began. "We're very different politically. He's very conservative, and I'm very liberal. But the things we do agree about are much more important; things like raising children, family, loving, responsibilities, and adventure. Any time, day or night, this man is a joy to be around."

Russell likewise was finding much in the complexity of Hawn that he loved. "Goldie is very intelligent, very aware, and yet she's also very womanly. She combines the two qualities of femininity and strength very well. She can be very strong, and yet she also likes being a girl. I like that a lot. That's real."

The first few days apart found Russell and Hawn throwing themselves into their work. But it was obvious they were happy in the growing belief that they had found their ideal life partner. The end of their respective workdays found them in long telephone conversations in which they reaffirmed their love.

Sensing that their relationship was for the long haul, they were determined not to allow it to cool while they were working at opposite ends of the country, even if it meant chalking up a lot of frequent-flier miles.

On weekends when neither of them had to work, Russell would hop a red-eye flight, and Goldie, in Los Angeles, would do the same. They would meet halfway across country in Dallas, Texas, and spend the weekend together before flying back in time for the Monday-morning first shot on their respective films. When she had to work on Saturdays, Russell would fly out to Los Angeles, spend Sunday with his love, and return to Miami in time to resume filming on Monday. They agreed that it was tough, but felt it was the thing you did when you were in love.

Meanwhile, *Protocol* was shaping up as an enjoyable experience for Goldie. She had a solid director in Herbert Ross, and the story line, while containing much broad-based humor, seemed a comfortable fit for Hawn, who admitted that the film was going over old ground and running counter to her desire to expand into serious, relevant work. When talking about the consequence of continuing to do the things people expected her to do, Goldie seemed inclined to finally stop fighting the stereotype.

"How do I not abandon a certain kind of feeling I might give an audience while still branching out to other movies?" she questioned. "There are certain things people want to see me do and certain things I'd like to do. The reason I get a lot of money to do pictures is not because I do what I want to do but because what I do has a tendency to lift the spirits. And you don't want to pull that out from under anybody."

Protocol finally finished the U.S. portion of filming and with a break before resuming in Tunisia, Goldie seized the opportunity to fly to Miami with the children and spend an extended period of time with Kurt.

Their obvious passion was very much on display during the days Goldie spent on the set of *Mean Season,* watching her man work. In one all-night filming session, Russell, playing a reporter in a cat-and-mouse game with a serial killer, is in a tense conversation with a fellow reporter. It was a long, expository scene that required many takes. Goldie, quite content, sat demurely at a table offstage, knitting.

The moment the director yelled cut, her prim and proper nature changed. She was up in a flash and ran to Russell's side, throwing her arms around his neck and kissing him hard on the mouth. It was a long and passionate kiss that bordered on the extremely intimate. Crew members walked around the couple as they clinched, trying hard not to notice the heat the pair was generating but finding it impossible not to.

When lunch was called at an ungodly early-morning hour, the pair disappeared into Kurt's trailer. The production assistant assigned to dog Kurt's footsteps and to get him where he had to be on time was in a bind. How could he knock on the trailer door when it was time to resume shooting when it was obvious that Goldie and Kurt were in the throes of passion? Magically, just as filming was about to resume, the trailer door opened. Russell and Hawn exited with big smiles on their faces, not making any pretense about what had just gone on inside. They displayed one last kiss before Kurt went back to the set and Goldie back to knitting.

"Watch Kurt!" Goldie said excitedly a few days later as she was watching her lover in a tense sequence in which he attacks a newspaper delivery man with a baseball bat. "He's so cute! He's so funny!" This day, Goldie was very much the giggling little girl.

There was more to this passionate stay in Miami than love and lust. Their time together was also about cementing the element of trust, especially as it pertained to her children and the man who had come into her life. Goldie had found, through their conversations and by watching him interact with Oliver and Kate as well as his own son, Boston that Russell was a man in every possible way.

"Life is fabulous with them [children]," said Russell, who had summertime custody of his son. "Being a father is not a burden. It's important for them [children] to wake up and know you're down the hall. If you love your kids, they'll love you back."

Hawn and Russell were up-front about the nature of their relationship and made it very plain to their children. When Russell, in a concession to the time-honored tradition of a wedding ring, presented Goldie with a diamond-encrusted "love ring," the couple decided to turn the gift into a ceremony involving the entire family. And so, not long after their relationship had taken its serious turn, Goldie and Kurt gathered Oliver, Kate, and Boston into their bedroom, where the children watched, smiling and wide-eyed, as they expressed their love for each other while Kurt slipped the ring on Goldie's finger.

Because of Kurt's strong paternal instinct, Goldie had no problem leaving Oliver, Kate, and their nanny with Russell when she flew to Tunisia to finish *Protocol*. It was the right decision. For the first time, Russel was interacting with the children without Goldie's presence and was strengthening what already appeared to be a sturdy bond. Goldie was happy her children were getting to know her man on a one-on-one basis. She missed her kids and wished she could be a fly on the wall when Kurt and the kids were together. But she knew that whatever was going on, it was good.

In April 1984, *Swing Shift* opened and was roundly criticized as being a mixture of ideas that ultimately added up to a confusing and distracting, rather than entertaining, experience. Hawn, who had been expecting the worst, was not surprised and renewed her promise that on future projects she would call the shots.

Goldie returned to the States after the completion of *Protocol* and jumped right back into her loving, family-oriented life with Russell. To this point their respective children had been in transition, jumping back and forth between California and Colorado. But now, secure in their relationship, Goldie and Kurt began more serious nesting.

Together they purchased seventy acres of prime Colorado land, in a place called Old Snowmass, which had lain undeveloped for years. Amid the dirt roads, rolling hills, and rivers, they began to build. First up was a guest house on one side of the property. On the other, Russell began supervising the construction of a large, log-framed house that would serve as the permanent family residence.

Once again Goldie and Kurt took some time for themselves, and once again it was abroad. The couple traveled extensively in India and Nepal and found serenity. Both actors had rabid international followings and were regularly mobbed in their travels. They took the lack of privacy on the trip in stride. At one point they looked at each other and Russell said, "Well, that takes care of Nepal and Thailand," and burst out laughing.

Kurt, as Goldie had by now discovered, was anything but the typical aggressive Hollywood actor. After completing *Mean Season*, he was quite content to supervise the building of their Colorado home, play with the kids, and be with Goldie. He would occasionally look at a script, but it would be the better part of a year before he would say yes to his next project. It was evident to Goldie that Kurt, unlike her two husbands, was not bothered in the least by the focus in the media on the fact that Goldie, once again, had more money, power, and fame than her significant other.

131

"Kurt and I are both very established, but we both have very different attitudes about the business. For Kurt it's a job, and he loves what he does. But he knows how fleeting this business can be, and so his attitude is What's the sense of destroying a relationship if you know the truth about your circumstances? Work is just an isolated part of his life. That's why we get along so well."

On the difference in their level of professional success, Russell has always been more direct. "I'm more of a hired gun. Goldie has taken time in investing in her career, whereas I don't get that involved. She enjoys the process of developing projects. I'm lazier. I'd rather just get a phone call and go to work."

Protocol hit theaters in December 1984. As with *Swing Shift*, the film got decidedly mixed reviews and only passable box office. But Goldie was not in the frame of mind to express more than temporary disappointment. "I wish it had gone through the roof, but it didn't. Most films don't."

And the reason *Protocol*'s failure did not drive her up a wall was that, after years of trying to balance career and relationships, Goldie appeared to have finally found happiness on both fronts. But as she closed in on her fortieth birthday, she suddenly saw that the picture was not complete. She wanted to have one more baby, with Kurt, and she was pretty sure that he would go for the idea of having a child that was theirs alone.

Russell had always been big on the topic of children. In fact, the man of few words would go on forever about the mundane things he had done with Boston that day or where he had taken Oliver or Kate. And in the recent past he had been more than willing to speculate on the question of children with Goldie.

"We talk about more family, and we're at a point where we have to make a decision about it," he said. "But you have to take a look at things and say what's right at this time in your life and what will be right in the near future. We're asking ourselves those questions right now, and we'll figure it out."

Their discussions about having a child ran the gamut from outlandish, with Russell once saying, "We'd like to have five or six more kids," to the realistic, with acknowledgment that Goldie was close to the end of her reproductive years. Goldie ultimately had the final word on the subject when she said she wanted to have one more baby for Kurt and for her family.

"I love Kurt very much. And it's hard on him because he only has his son with him part of the time. So I wanted to have a baby for him...and for my children. To watch their mother get pregnant would be a great education. They would be thrilled watching my stomach grow."

Russell could only marvel at her logic. Faced with that kind of unselfish argument, Russell could do nothing else but agree, and early in 1985 the couple was happily engaged in trying to increase the size of their family.

"We really wanted to have a child together because we wanted to see what we'd have," said Russell, ever ready to cast the decision in the lightest possible way. "We just couldn't deny the instinct of saying, 'Let's make babies.' We were both getting to an age where the decision had to be made, and so we made it."

The idea of making a baby made an already excellent physical relationship that much more exciting and urgent. During the ensuing weeks and months it would take very little prompting to get the couple behind closed doors.

Hawn, however, was never far from a pile of scripts vying for her attention. She was not surprised at the types of things she was being offered: frothy, over-the-top comedies in which her character invariably laughed and mugged her way through outlandish situations and daring adventures to a happy ending. But one script, *Wildcats,* struck her fancy.

The film related the totally improbable tale of a naive female physical-education teacher who is stuck with the job of coaching an undisciplined, all-male, inner-city high school football team. *Wildcats* contained many of the conventions associated with television sitcoms as the coach slowly but surely rounds the team into a cohesive unit and finally leads them to the championship. Goldie saw the character of the coach, even in her more physical moments, as somebody she could play without too much stress and strain. She also saw *Wildcats* as something she wanted a direct hand in and so she willingly assumed the role of executive producer title and all the logistical and financial responsibilities that went along with the job.

Goldie wanted *Wildcats,* despite its rather improbable storyline, to be believable in a physical and football sense, and so she hired a real football coach to give her a grueling physical workout that emphasized such skills as blocking, tackling, and other elements of the gridiron sport. Hawn emerged physically fit and ready for action.

For Goldie, *Wildcats* turned out to be a walk in the park. In action director Michael Ritchie's practiced hands, she got to play tomboy, running around football fields, bumping into people and things, falling down, and yelling a lot. The cast members, which included Swoosie Kurtz and bit player and rising rap star L L Cool J, immediately bonded. The knowledge that they were not making great art kept things loose and friendly.

Kurt and the children would make occasional visits to the *Wildcats* set. Russell, no slouch when it came to athletics, was a cheerleader on the sidelines when Goldie would step in the middle of a group of big actors in football outfits and get in their faces, yelling encouragement and occasional obscenities in keeping with the manly sport. It was not uncommon for Goldie, after the completion of a particularly rigorous scene, to come running, coated in mud, into Kurt's arms. (During those visits, the couple would inevitably find time to steal away for some baby making.)

While she willingly conformed to yet another comic role, Goldie was continuing to have a crisis of conscience. "It's frustrating," she admitted one day between football shots. "Part of me wants to stretch out and do other things, and the other part doesn't want to abandon the road I've laid in comedy."

In the meantime, getting pregnant continued to be high on their list of things to do. But what Kurt and Goldie were not entertaining was the thought that they would get married anytime soon. In response to the marriage question, Hawn stated, "At the moment we don't want to. Kurt has bought me a beautiful ring as a symbol of our love, and any child we have will be getting the name Russell."

Russell claimed that their reluctance to make their relationship legal was the result, in part, of their collective failed marriages. "Goldie and I talk about marriage from time to time. Marriage is something we're old-fashioned about and wish we could have for each other. But it's something we were both involved in before, and it didn't work out for either of us. When that happens, the word marriage sort of leaves a bad taste in your mouth. We're already a family, so it's not necessary."

The couple's drive to conceive continued through the winter and summer months. Goldie would regularly run into Kurt's arms and announce excitedly that she was pregnant. They would just as quickly discover that it was a false alarm. Goldie was getting discouraged.

"We really wanted that baby," Russell remembered, "and we had been trying for about eight months. Goldie must have come to me at least seven times saying, 'I think I'm pregnant.' Finally, I sat down with her and said, 'Let's try to do this right.' So we figured out what her best days were to conceive."

Goldie became pregnant in November 1985, and with *Wildcats* finally completed, she settled happily into the role of mother-to-be. She spent much of her complication-free pregnancy in her Pacific Palisades home, driving Oliver to and from school, chasing after Kate and her dog, Thumper, and when he was home, living the good life with Kurt. During those months, Goldie marveled at the fact that being pregnant at age forty was a totally different experience.

"I do have a deeper understanding of what I'm doing than I did when I was younger," she reflected. "I'm even more romantic about it now than I was then. It's a true miracle. It's really an extraordinary feeling. Knowing this will be my last pregnancy, I'm savoring it. In fact, the only regret I have is that I didn't meet Kurt sooner so that we could have more children together."

Entering the new year, Goldie and Kurt had begun spending more and more time at the developing Old Snowmass compound. The kids and occasionally Goldie's mother would join them. For Goldie, the time away from Hollywood was a period of major adjustment. Accustomed to life in the big city, she was shocked to find out just how remote Old Snowmass was. It took a twenty-mile jeep ride to get to Aspen, and some of the roads were extremely bumpy.

135

Goldie was missing telephone calls because the primitive hookup they had did not always work. To get their mail, they had to drive a half hour to the nearest post office. But those were minor obstacles for Goldie, who, not surprisingly, was looking on the bright side. "Moving here has been good for us, especially the children. It's such a pleasure to be away from the business. I tend to go crazy being in the midst of everything. I love my work, but if I do too much of it, it's suddenly not fun anymore."

During this first extended Colorado stay, Goldie was content to do the simple things: supervising the children, decorating the cabin, and slowly, often unpleasantly, coming to grips with the fact that Kurt was a hunter, one who would often return with game that would have to be cooked and eaten. She initially turned her nose up at what Kurt brought home but eventually changed her attitude and begin spending hours at the wood-burning stove, making impressive wildlife feasts.

Kurt was also in a period of self-imposed unemployment and was content with riding the flatlands in his jeep, playing with the children, and doing the occasional good deed for one of his handful of neighbors. Most of all, he marveled at how Goldie the workaholic had learned to slow down.

"Sure she needs a creative outlet," he explained. "But one of the things I've been able to teach her is how to relax. She's always done a lot of work because she has a lot of energy. What I've tried to do is to get her to channel that energy into things other than the moviemaking."

Wildcats was released on February 14, 1986. While conceding that the film was good fun, critics also lobbed a few grenades in the direction of its predictability. Goldie, with fond memories of making the film, was not going to let those barbs pass without some rebuttal. "*Wildcats* is not the kind of movie you can critique," said Hawn as she strained against the pressure of her expanding stomach. "You have to go to a theater, see people laughing, and say, 'This movie is fun.' We made this picture specifically for people to have a good time with."

The excitement surrounding the upcoming birth of their child carried Goldie and Kurt through the beginning of the summer. Despite the increasing discomfort of morning sickness and swollen ankles, she continued to be radiant and upbeat.

Although they had been offered the opportunity, neither parent had expressed the desire to know ahead of time the sex of their child. That it would come into the world healthy was all they cared to know.

Russell did not want to be far from home with Goldie so close to giving birth. But the coming release of his film *Big Trouble in Little China* forced him to fly to New York to help publicize the film. During those days away, Kurt was as nervous as an expectant father could possibly be. He did his best to concentrate on the work at hand, but Goldie was always on his mind.

During the endless round of press interviews, he would constantly slip away for a quick phone call home. And when reporters, privy to their coming blessed event, would ask Kurt how he felt, he would nervously laugh and admit to wishing he was back home. But *Big Trouble in Little China* was a John Carpenter film, and Carpenter films were a notoriously hard sell, and so Russell patiently talked up the film until the last reporter was out the door. He was right behind that reporter and on the next flight back to Los Angeles.

Adding to the stress in the days prior to Goldie's giving birth was the unexpected announcement by Russell's ex-wife, Season Hubley, that she had retained legal counsel and was considering taking Kurt back to court for an increase in his $2,000-a-month child-support payments. "I know Goldie's kids go to private school," reported Hubley as she went public with her request. "I want the best for my child, and Kurt should want that, too." Even while threatening to drag her ex-husband back into court, Hubley still found time to offer congratulations. "I'm excited for Kurt and Goldie, and I wish only the best for their child." The child-support issue was finally settled, although no dollar figures were announced.

Kurt and Goldie celebrated the Fourth of July in a fairly subdued manner with family, a few friends, and some fireworks. Given the doctor's assurance that Goldie could go into labor at any moment,

Kurt was nervous. He tried not to hover, but as the day drew closer, he made a point of not being far from home for very long. The bags under their eyes were mute evidence that neither of them had been sleeping well.

Goldie went into labor on July 10, 1986. With Kurt at her side, she was wheeled into the delivery room. Moments later, Wyatt Hawn Russell came into the world. "I cut his cord," Kurt would relate later. "It was pretty exciting." Goldie described the experience this way: "It was very bloody and scary. I think Kurt has seen my entire insides."

Goldie, still in her postbirth euphoria, recalled: "I saw the testicles, and I screamed, 'It's not a girl! It's a man!'"

Prior to getting pregnant, Goldie had dropped hints that she was once again considering taking some time off. "But with the birth of Wyatt, I'm definitely ready for a break. I've been working real hard for the past couple of years, and I'm totally depleted."

Goldie spent the rest of 1986 being the stay-at-home mom, making trips to Colorado with Russell (who, following the release of his 1986 films *Big Trouble in Little China* and *The Best of Times,* was also taking a break) and supervising the ongoing construction of the family's sprawling ranch house. Her mother was a regular visitor to their Pacific Palisades home and was drawing strength and immense joy from being around her grandchildren and Kurt's son.

Wyatt's infancy was a happy time on top of already happy times. But while totally committed to the children and family life, Goldie and Kurt still maintained the keen instincts of lovers. They were aware of each other's look or touch that said, We need to be alone or we need to get away for a while. Although not legally married, they introduced each other as "my husband" and "my wife."

Their bond was obviously strong, but what many failed to realize was the degree to which Kurt had surrendered his heart, soul, and emotional being to Goldie. This became evident not too long after the birth of Wyatt, when Kurt woke up from a terrible dream. In it, Goldie was dying, and Kurt was helpless to do anything about it except pray that he could join her in death so he would not have to be alone. "When I woke up from the dream, I was breathing hard and crying," he recalled of that painful experience. "That was fear. That was bad. It drove home the point that I don't like the idea of not being able to be with Goldie."

Goldie had likewise given herself over to Kurt and, in a very Russell-like way, was succinct in summing up their relationship. "We live together, we love together, we think together, and we have a family together."

But work together? As joyous an experience as *Swing Shift* had been, neither had given any indication that they were anxious to work together again real soon. Since becoming involved with Kurt, Goldie had often stated that she would "never mix my career with love." Nevertheless, in early 1987 the arrival of the script for *Overboard* presented just such an opportunity.

Overboard told the story of a wealthy, spoiled woman who falls off a yacht, is washed ashore, and awakens in a hospital, where she is claimed by a carpenter and his pack of unruly kids. Like all the scripts Goldie was being offered at the time, it adhered to a formula of broad comedy, good-natured laughs, and sight gags. In the script stage it came across as lighter than air. But when first Goldie and then Kurt read it, they thought, recalled Hawn, Gee! This is fun! In particular, she saw the heart in the story, immediately elevating this bit of fluff to something worth doing. "I know this is comedy," she said in her assessment of *Overboard*. "But I didn't relate to it as if it would be making a joke. Kurt and I believe in the rewards of family, and so we like this script for that reason."

Their thoughts never too far from their children. Russell and Hawn liked the idea that *Overboard* would be filmed in California locations, allowing them the luxury of having their children with them.

Director Garry Marshall went into *Overboard* with mixed emotions. A looming directors' strike was dividing his loyalties. "One of my main reasons for agreeing to do *Overboard* was that M-G-M promised to pay me very well. I also wanted to direct a romantic comedy. But the thing that cinched the deal for me was that Goldie was attached to the project. I always found her hilarious, sexy, and lovable and had always dreamed of working with her on something."

Marshall, however, was savvy enough to realize that there were potential pitfalls in starring real-life lovers as film lovers. To avoid any potential awkwardness, he started off the first day of filming on *Overboard* by putting Russell and Hawn in bed in a scene that was originally scheduled for later in the shoot. The pair immediately warmed to the irony and laughed and giggled their way through the scene, effectively breaking the ice and setting *Overboard* on a positive course. And it was not long before Marshall saw the advantage of having lovers acting together.

"Goldie's doing some good stuff," said the director of those first days filming on the northern California coast. "In fact, this may be Goldie's finest performance, and a lot has to do with the fact that Kurt is here. The chemistry between them is incredible. The very first time they kiss, you certainly get the feeling they've done it before. One thing I've noticed is that Goldie, in many of her pictures, has had nobody to really react against. But when she's bouncing off Kurt, she's at her best."

His obvious acting abilities aside, Russell's presence on the set continued to exert a calming influence on Hawn. Between takes the couple would often be spotted hugging, giggling, and kissing. When things were not going right and Hawn was having trouble nailing a scene, Kurt could be counted on to make her laugh. When Wyatt would have a rough night and Goldie would not get much sleep, Russell would come to the set early to ask Marshall to shoot his scenes first so that Goldie could get a couple of extra hours.

The homey feel was helped by the fact that Oliver, eleven, Kate, eight, and Wyatt, now an active one-year-old, were always on the set, the older children frolicking on the beach while Wyatt, in the charge of the ever-vigilant nanny, crawled, rolled, and cooed on a blanket just out of camera range, where he would occasionally cause the motherly side of Goldie to overrule the acting side.

"What was that?" Goldie started one day, stopping a scene with Kurt in mid-sentence. She turned in the direction of Marshall, who shrugged his shoulders and said he had not hear a thing. But Goldie was insistent.

"That cough," insisted Goldie, her face drawing up into a look of concern. "I think it was the baby." She ran from the set to the spot where the nanny, with Wyatt in her arms, was watching. She was gone for several minutes before returning to the set, a sheepish grin on her face. She assured Kurt and Marshall that Wyatt was fine. "Oh, yes," she said giggling. "Where were we."

One day the *Overboard* cast and crew were at the Long Beach, California, harbor, filming a scene in which Goldie's character, dressed in a sleeveless gold evening gown, had to jump into ice-cold water with a life preserver around her and swim around. During the course of the day, Goldie willingly shot the wet, cold, uncomfortable scene twice. "But unfortunately I didn't get the shot," recalled the director, "because we kept losing the camera angle. So we had to shoot the scene again."

He could tell that Goldie, sitting shivering on the shore, would not be thrilled. His worst fears came to pass when he half-jokingly informed her that she would have to jump into the water one more time. "No! No! No!" she yelled. "It's freezing out there! I don't want to go back in the water! I'm done!"

Marshall was in a quandary. He understood why Goldie did not want to do it again. But they needed that shot, and the light was starting to slip away. The crew stood by as the director attempted to come up with something that would persuade the star of the film to get cold and wet. It was at that moment that Russell, already on Marshall's good-guy list for such small niceties as helping the crew move equipment, once again came to the rescue.

Russell went over to Hawn, hugged and kissed her, and then hit her with a dose of reality. "Goldie, for the money you're getting to do this picture, you've got to jump into the water right now."

She looked at Russell, her face turned into a frown and just as quickly into a smile of resignation. "Oh, you're right," she said with a sigh. "She went over to Marshall, informed him that she was ready to do the scene, jumped in the water, and proceeded to swim around for an hour and a half.

With the completion of *Overboard*, Hawn and Russell returned to a period of domestic bliss. The trips to Colorado became more frequent and protracted as the main house was nearing completion.

Hawn was taking a real shine to frontier life. She was becoming increasingly adept at turning the game Kurt brought back from his hunting trips into imaginative dishes. She began planting vegetables and ended up with what Russell described as a "significant" garden. And she was understanding when Kurt would disappear for a few days to hunt, fish, or to just be alone.

"Goldie has adapted rather well," said Russell. "She was brought up in a pretty rural area of Maryland, and so she was never what you would call a big-city girl. She has always had a desire to live the way we do, and she's happy with the time she spends here."

Happy was not the operative word back in Hollywood, where Marshall was in postproduction hell on *Overboard*. The film, in its preproduction stage, had gone through an evolution of sorts. Initially, the film was supposed to center on the relationship between a mother and her children. But it was decided, once Hawn and Russell were cast, that the project would be better served with a love story to balance things out. Consequently the *Overboard* that Marshall shot had the agreeable tag of lighthearted, romantic family comedy.

"M-G-M, however, was not charmed with my finished product," the director lamented. "It turns out that they wanted an adult movie they could market to a sophisticated audience. At that point I didn't have much clout, and so they sent me back to the editing room with instructions to cut down the film and push the relationship between Goldie and Kurt. I ended up trimming all of the character's back stories, and so I was left with a lot of characters who look like sticks."

Following *Overboard*, Goldie took a long, hard look at her career. She felt a strong need to control her own destiny and to do different kinds of work. And she also had to come to terms with the fact that she had participated in the very stereotyping she had so vehemently fought. Her last three films had been near carbon copies of each other as she continued to play the wide-eyed innocent that had marked her entrance into show business.

Hawn was clearly at odds with herself on this subject, and the frustration began manifesting itself in often terse replies. "I guess I could be considered terminally cute," she conceded. "But what difference does it make. I mean, what's so threatening about that kind of personality?"

On the strength of *Private Benjamin* and *Swing Shift,* Goldie could have pressed the issue as producer and made her own rules. But there was a basic insecurity in her that often had her passing the baton of responsibility to another producer. However, Goldie had nobody but herself to blame when it came to *Protocol,* which reflected her choices as both a producer and an actor.

When it came out in December 1987, *Overboard* continued to perpetuate the stereotype that had made Goldie Hawn a bankable, star-level commodity. That her first postrelationship work with Russell failed was a particularly crushing blow.

"It was the biggest disappointment I ever had," she said, speaking more from the heart and ignoring the reality that the truncated *Overboard* deserved its mixed reviews and mediocre box office. "It's like having a big fish on the end of the line, you bring it up, and it kind of wiggles off the hook. We were both very depressed, but we went on. We looked at the reviews, I made dinner, and we went on and had our life."

But Goldie was hurting. The frustration of a career that suddenly seemed mired in mediocrity was almost getting too painful to discuss.

"You can't make a good movie every time out," said Hawn when asked to explain the lackluster showings of her last three films. "Nobody can. Maybe I made the wrong choices. There could be a million reasons why those films didn't work.

"But I just don't know what happened."

11

Tough Enough

THE CHANCES WERE REAL GOOD THAT IF YOU WERE LOOKING for Goldie Hawn between 1987 and 1990, you would most likely spot her running after or with her kids. After the failure of *Overboard,* Hawn went into a self-imposed hiatus, spending her days supervising improvements on both the Pacific Palisades and Colorado homes and shuttling her kids to dance classes and sporting events.

Goldie was reveling in the simple pleasures of being a wife and mother, going places and doing things with her mother and sister, and experiencing all the simple pleasures of life. "Figuring out what's for dinner is a big deal," she related at the time. "I'm always doing something. What I'm finding out is that being a mother, there is no downtime."

By contrast, Russell's phone began to ring off the hook with offers, and as Goldie's professional life retreated into the background, he became superbusy. He landed the costarring role opposite Mel Gibson and Michelle Pfeiffer in *Tequila Sunrise* and the costarring role opposite Sylvester Stallone in the action film *Tango and Cash.* He also agreed to be part of the smaller, character-oriented film *The Winter People.* Goldie was thrilled with her lover's heavy workload, often citing Russell, with more than an aside to her previous husbands as an example of someone fully capable of carrying his share of the material load and dealing with the realities of everyday life.

Hawn, however, was not taking a complete sabbatical from show business. As always, she was on the lookout for new projects, particularly those that would take her beyond the Goldie stereotype. Unfortunately, she was finding little to her liking. She was frustrated that the scripts she was seeing were vintage Goldie Hawn vehicles—heavy on comedy and light on substance. She became even more determined to find a role for herself both behind and in front of the camera.

"Sometimes I wish I had tougher skin," she lamented of her inability to take control of her projects. "I have to start saying, 'This is the way things are going to go,.' and not worry about whether people are going to like me. I don't want to be the one to rise up monsterlike and always confront the director. But I think I'm finally getting there."

A true test of Goldie's toughness came in 1989 when her former husband Bill Hudson, after a period of silence during which he had gone on to marry actress Cindy Williams, began taking shots at his former wife in the press. Goldie had always insisted that her break with Hudson had been amicable, and she had stuck by the joint-custody arrangement in regard to their children. While there was still some residual bitterness surrounding the way Hudson had sprung the divorce on her, she continued to insist that her former husband was a wonderful father. So it came as a shock when she began reading the awful things Hudson was saying about her.

Especially when it came to Hudson's allegations that Goldie was making it difficult for him to see his own children. "I have alternate weekend visitation rights," proclaimed Hudson, "but that's only when they're in Los Angeles. When they're in town, I have them as often as I can. But Goldie travels a lot. She's a megastar, she flies around the world, and my kids are caught in this whirlwind with her. It's hard for me to plan anything with them as a family."

In comments to various publications, Hudson continued to press the issue. "My visitation rights are often ignored because

Goldie has the children in Aspen with Kurt Russell. I don't want to do battle with Goldie over the kids, but I don't want to have to chase them all over the country. I've asked her to let me have the children on a more regular basis, and she tells me she will think about it."

Hudson was also not above taking shots at Russell. "The agreement I have with Goldie is that I'm supposed to get the kids three days out of the week. But who do I call when Goldie's out of town? Kurt? What right does he have to tell me when I can see my kids?"

Hawn exploded upon reading these comments and quickly fired back with uncharacteristic anger. She alluded to the divorce settlement and the fact that Hudson got their Malibu house as a big part of it. "I'd pick up shit on the street before I'd ask someone for money." She continued to display her rarely seen vindictive side when she angrily launched into a counterattack on his charges. "His comments devastated the children. He's trying to make mincemeat out of me, the children, and Kurt."

Goldie claimed that Hudson's sudden bad-mouthing of her was a vendetta because she would not sign a document that would allow him to borrow money on the Malibu house. "He's still trying to live off me. If he really has a beef with me, let him call and face me like a man...not like a woman scorned."

Goldie's double-barrel blast at Hudson was a shock to many who had long ago dismissed her as an easygoing person who was above rolling around in the dirt. But what her exchange with Hudson had proved was that Hawn, largely out of frustration over the inability to be firm in her professional life, had developed a strong code of ethics which, in essence, said: "I won't mess with you, but if you mess with me, you're going to be sorry."

The battle with Hudson did cause her to privately reflect on just how scattered her personal life had been. "I've been through some terrible times in my life," she confessed. "I just can't seem to forget that I've had two marriages go down the drain. I don't suffer those memories daily, but I can see that I've paid big prices for my success."

Hawn's anger soon dissipated as her loving relationship with

Russell continued to only get better. That they were in sync with each other was without question. When she once told Kurt, in passing, that they should get away for a while, he surprised her with a three-day getaway in Hawaii. When he was not working, Russell's life revolved around Goldie and the children. With Goldie, talk would often center around business or what was going on in Wyatt's preschool. It was not uncommon for a visitor to the Pacific Palisades home to see a hot and sweaty Russell chasing after Oliver and his friends during an impromptu softball game as Goldie watched, beaming.

But as good as her life was, it was not enough for Hawn, who needed to work. The reality seemed to be that Goldie was going to die of old age waiting for a role that would totally change her image in people's eyes. Like many actors in Hollywood, she found herself taking the best available script rather than the best one.

Meanwhile, another Hollywood star was trying to break out of his own career straitjacket. Mel Gibson, after wading through what seemed like countless scripts in an attempt to at least temporarily shake his action image, found *Bird on a Wire,* which struck him as "a frothy piece of fun and action." While working on *Tequila Sunrise* with Kurt Russell, Gibson had met and become good friends with Goldie, and the two had expressed the hope of working together at some point.

In looking back on Goldie's decision to do *Bird on a Wire,* Russell teasingly took all the credit. "It's always been fun when I knew the guy Goldie was thinking of working with. So I told Goldie, 'I think you guys would make a great couple.'"

Once Goldie stopped laughing at Russell's cinematic matchmaking, she had to admit that working opposite the low-key macho, actor would be a hoot. Fortunately for Goldie, the list of leading ladies was never very long, and she was on or near the top of it.

The project came together rather quickly in late 1989, with Goldie very much on the mind of producer Rob Cohen. "We wanted Goldie because she was so blond, light, and funny. We knew Goldie, in combination with Mel Gibson, would have tremendous appeal." Gibson seconded the choice, citing "her spontaneity and sexiness."

Bird on a Wire offered up the tale of a man who has been hiding via the FBI's witness protection program. He gets dropped from protection, hooks up with his former girlfriend, and in short order is on the run from drug dealers. On the one hand, Goldie agreed that *Bird on a Wire* would not be great art; on the other, there appeared to be some substance among the chases, gunfire, and high-wire antics. "I saw it as a film that dealt with relationships that end at an early age and the 'what ifs' that come after," she explained. "I like that aspect of the script."

Throw in the fact that she would be doing the kind of action and stunts she had not really done since *Foul Play* and Goldie was hooked. In the wake of the relative failure of her recent star vehicles, what ultimately sold Hawn on the project was that she would not be under the lights alone. "I did not want to carry the total responsibility for a movie rising or falling."

But ever conscious of her image as an innocent, Hawn did have some problems with the draft of the script she had seen. There were a number of fairly graphic sex scenes built into the story that seemed out of place. "I saw the film as being about love, getting people together and remembering. I saw the whole thing as being quite innocent. It just wasn't right to see those two people go at it together. I felt, for the audience, it would be a turnoff."

Goldie immediately got on the phone with Gibson and nicely but firmly objected. "I told him the scenes were totally hot and heavy. Then I asked him, 'Have you ever seen me do a love scene? It's just not my thing.'" Gibson agreed and had the offending scenes either softened or cut out all together.

Bird on a Wire turned out to be a summer-camp kind of filmmaking experience. Director John Badham, a practiced hand when it came to action films, was quick to latch on to Hawn's physicality and over-the-top, broad-based approach to acting and incorporated those strengths into many of her scenes.

Gibson was everything she could hope for in a costar. He was always up for laughs or a practical joke in between filming and turned out to be a fair amateur magician. Goldie spent a lot of her downtime sitting quietly, knitting clothes for Wyatt. There was a lot

(*Right*) Goldie and
Kurt in 1989 (Scott
Downie) (All pictures
courtesy Celebrity
Photo)

(*Below*) Goldie with
her son Oliver and
Kurt in 1991 (Janet
Gough)

(*Above*) Goldie in 1992
(Craig Skinner)

(*Left*) Goldie in 1995

(*Above*) Goldie, with Diane Keaton and Bette Midler at the premiere of *The First Wives' Club* on September 16, 1996 (Kevin Winter)

(*Right*) Goldie with her three children, Kate, Oliver, and Wyatt, at *The First Wives' Club* premiere

(*Above*) Goldie in 1995
(Stephen Trupp)

(*Left*) With Liza Minnelli
(Scott Downie)

of good-natured give-and-take between Goldie and Mel, and with no controversy for the press to sink their teeth into, the gossip columns began cranking out the old notion that Goldie was once again falling in love with her costar. She saw the absurdity in the reports but quickly put an end to any speculation that might get back to Kurt and the children.

"My relationship with Kurt is solid," she reported. "Why would I have a romance with anybody else? I'm already in love. I have the best guy around."

The good-time nature of the shoot was fueled by the fact that Russell, not working at the time, was able to put his flying expertise to good use by piloting the children up to the *Bird on a Wire* set for regular visits. "I'm one of the few actors who actually enjoys being on someone else's location," offered Russell of the businessman's holiday. "During one visit, Mel's wife and kids were there, and we all got together during nonshooting time and went to parks and boating and had a whole lot of fun."

The running, jumping, dodging gunfire, and hanging from high places that were a constant on the film was just the tonic for Goldie to show that her forty-four-year-old body had not lost a step. She loved the action-packed finale in which she and Gibson ran through a zoo as bullets whizzed all around them. Another scene, in which Gibson and she had to crawl across a girder twenty stories above the street, also stuck in her mind. "I was in this gown that was all satin and weighed about forty pounds, and my knees kept catching under it. I didn't dare look down."

She also remembered the day they were crawling around on a ledge, again twenty stories above the ground. Everything had gone fine for a number of takes, and the director had just launched into another when Goldie's longtime fear of heights suddenly and unexpectedly kicked in. She froze, began to sway, and started to fall. Gibson lunged for her, grabbed her by the arms, and hauled her off the ledge and to safety. When she recovered her composure, Goldie proclaimed to anyone who would listen, "Make no mistake. Mel saved my life."

Goldie was very much in her element during the filming of *Bird on a Wire*. On the set, she was on top of things and aware of herself. When a scene was finished, it was not uncommon for Hawn to walk over to director Badham and say, "I'm not jumping up and down about that one." The result was that she would often get that second and third take and would come away from the conference secure in the knowledge that she had nailed it. Gibson was also well aware of his costar's diligence and contributions on the set. "Goldie added some great ideas to our relationship in the film."

When she had the time, she would often be on the phone, talking deals and discussing upcoming projects. And just as often, she would hang up after a long and arduous business call and open her refrigerator just to gaze at the picture of her kids smiling out at her that she had hung inside.

The star-driven *Bird on a Wire* opened in 1990 with a critical thud. And rightfully so. The story line, which had been admittedly suspect in the script stage, was downright ludicrous on the screen. The promised chemistry between Hawn and Gibson was more frantic posturing and mugging than real interaction. For an action picture, *Bird on a Wire* was finally boring and predictable.

Hawn took some particularly hard hits from the critics, receiving none-too-veiled references to the fact that her innocent, giggly-girl image was not aging well. But that did not stop audiences from flocking to the film and, when the dust settled, not only making it Goldie's best box-office effort since *Private Benjamin* but showing the Hollywood naysayers, in no uncertain terms, that Goldie still meant gold.

As was her pattern, Goldie immediately put her professional success behind her and went back to the domestic life she so loved. Wyatt, now four years old, was at the scattered, questioning, running-around stage and demanded Goldie's constant attention. Visitors to her home began to find the common sight of Goldie, out of breath, her hair flying in all directions, chasing Wyatt around the house or through the backyard.

Goldie had forgotten what it was like to have a small child in her life, but when she had a moment to reflect, she agreed that the process of mothering a young child was worth doing again. "This is my third child and my last," she remarked. "Each one you treasure more, and this one I'm treasuring the most."

Goldie was also discovering more reasons to appreciate Kurt. Sometimes it was the little things, like his giving up a quiet day at home to chauffeur the kids. Sometimes he would ask her if she wanted to get away for a few days and then whisk her off to some secret love nest. Most of the time, it was just his being there when she woke up.

It was a relationship that continued to be the talk and envy of Hollywood. Longtime friend Cher said, "They have the best relationship of anybody I know. Kurt is perfect, and Goldie has a really good heart. Whatever it is they have, it works." Another longtime friend, actress Gail Strickland, said, "I've seen it all. I've spent cranky time with them and long, wonderful family time with them."

Strickland also had a front-row seat during the continuing skirmishes between Hawn and ex-husband Hudson. "I know the situation with Hudson continues to be one of the saddest things in her life. But Goldie is just refusing to live in anger and pain."

Goldie acknowledged those same sentiments. "I have no malice. I feel it's deeply important to forgive people."

Russell knew enough to stay out of that portion of Goldie's life, offering an ear to her latest stories of her battles with her ex and, if asked, offering some advice. But he never got actively involved. That was not his style.

It was during the post-*Bird* period that Goldie's production company spread its wings still wider as Hawn and Anthea Sylbert undertook their first coexecutive production deal without Goldie in front of the camera with the film *My Blue Heaven*. The film, a lighthearted comedy about an organized-crime figure trying to go straight in suburbia, seemed solid on paper. It did not hurt that Steve Martin was set to play the lead and Hawn favorite Herbert Ross would direct. What did hurt was that the script was always in a state of rewrites throughout preproduction and well into actual filming. Consequently *My Blue Heaven*, released in 1990, was occasionally funny, but mostly not, and had the reviews and poor box office that it deserved.

In 1990, Goldie reunited with *Laugh-In* creator George Schlatter to sing and dance her way through a television tribute to Sammy Davis Jr. For Goldie, it was as if she had stepped into a time warp and returned to her first days on *Laugh-In,* forgetting her lines and song lyrics during rehearsals and reducing Schlatter to hysterics. "Your forgetting lines is how I got to Beverly Hills," he told her. "If you had remembered them, we'd both be living in the Valley and driving a pickup truck."

Disney Studios, as it turned out, had been watching Goldie quite closely. With the memory of her triumph at the helm of *Private Benjamin* and the recent success of *Bird on a Wire,* they conveniently forgot the lean years in between and, in what industry insiders considered a daring move, signed Goldie to a seven-picture deal, worth approximately $30 million in 1991.

For Goldie, there was a lot to like in the deal. It was heavy on development and producing perks and would allow her to do outside projects at other studios. With the critical barbs of *Bird on a Wire* still on her mind, Goldie was grateful that Disney put the deal together with an eye toward allowing her to branch out. "Disney wants me to stretch my entire range as an actress. Which is good because as you get older, the parts get scarcer, and the question becomes: Do I abandon my image or not? This deal will allow me to change."

Hawn was doing more than talking about change. The ink had barely dried on the Disney deal when Goldie began to champion two dramatic adult scripts called *Last Wish* and *Babe West.* She was attracted to the notion that both stories featured world-weary women and that, while there were comedic moments, the emphasis was very much on drama. But to her dismay Goldie found, as she attempted to get financial and studio backing for these projects, that money people were reluctant to back any project that did not feature the trademark funny Goldie Hawn.

Disney was immediately feeling the heat. That they did not fall all over themselves to sign their new franchise player to do both films was looking bad in the press. They would have to move fast to repair the damage.

Hawn found out firsthand how deeply entrenched her image, even at age forty-five, was when she got wind of a feminist-themed buddy project about two women forced by circumstances into a life of crime. Hawn fell in love with the project, called *Thelma & Louise*. Her agent at the time, Ron Meyer, did not want her to do it, citing his moral problems with the script.

Undaunted, Goldie arranged for a meeting with *Thelma & Louise* director Ridley Scott. The meeting was cordial, but Scott, in a backhanded compliment, turned Hawn down on the grounds that he was afraid that her star status would overshadow the script. Goldie was disappointed, but, in hindsight she understood Scott's reasoning. "Parts like that [*Thelma & Louise*] don't come along that often, and I'm not usually considered for them. They don't want to deal with the baggage. They think the focus will be on me rather than the movie."

While disappointed, Goldie remained steadfast in turning down the inevitable rush of paper-thin scripts coming her way. "I've been in so many films where I was the woman in a man's world that I decided after *Wildcats* that I would just refuse to do those kinds of films anymore."

Disney was also continuing to do its part to try to make Goldie happy, plunking down a reported $175,000 for the rights to a script, called *Mrs. Faust*, in which a small-town woman must decide whether to sell her soul to the devil. *Mrs. Faust* had more drama than laughs going for it, but as often happens in Hollywood, the enthusiasm for the script soon waned, and within a year the script found itself mired in a development morass from which to date it has not reemerged.

Goldie finally found the change-of-pace film for the first project in her Disney deal in the suspense tale called *The Mrs.* The script told the story of a happily married New York woman who discovers after her husband is murdered that he was not the man she thought he was. She liked the tension and unexpected thrills that leaped off the script's pages and loved the idea of playing a strong woman and a survivor.

In line with her experimental attitude, Goldie passed on A-list directors in favor of a relative unknown, Damian Harris, and solid actors, like John Heard and Kate Reid. Disney executives looked at *The Mrs.* with some reservations, wishing privately that the film was not quite so dark, that the director had a little more experience, and that the character Goldie would play was not totally unlike the familiar image audiences had of her.

But it would have been a public-relations nightmare to air those concerns in light of the magnitude of the deal they had struck with her, and so Disney crossed its corporate fingers as *The Mrs.* prepared to go before the cameras. The film ultimately turned into yet another jumble of creative and personal nightmares.

At around this time, Goldie and Bill Hudson became engaged in another round of custody battles. Hudson evoked a technicality stating that either she or Russell had to be in the house with the children at all times. With Kurt already hard at work on the movie *Backdraft*, Goldie was forced to postpone the starting date of *The Mrs.* for several months. Goldie, remarked with an ironic sigh "I regret that I didn't spend more time getting to know him [Hudson]."

Meanwhile, trouble was brewing between the film's writer, Mary Agnes Donoghue, and its director. Donoghue was asked to make changes she was not comfortable with and so declined to rewrite the script. Another writer was quickly brought in.

While keeping tabs on the progress of *The Mrs.*, Goldie made a number of visits with the children to the *Backdraft* set. While Kurt would spend his days running in and out of burning buildings, Goldie would watch in wide-eyed wonder as her man risked fiery death in the name of believability. It was during one of those visits that the gossip columns burned with reports of loud arguing and screaming coming from Goldie and Kurt's hotel room. The cynics ran with these reports and predicted that their relationship was on the rocks.

Jami Way, Russell's sister, had a good laugh at those reports. "They may well have been fighting. They're a normal couple and Kurt can get pretty exasperating at times."

Russell also got wind of the reports and was annoyed. "Our relationship isn't a fairyland. We get angry at each other and we struggle over things like the kids. We are very much like most families."

Goldie giggled when the news of their apparent conflict got back to her. "Maybe what they heard was us making love."

Backdraft finally completed principal photography and Goldie was free to start *The Mrs.* But what she discovered was that the project was slowly beginning to unravel.

Disney could not remain silent too long after filming began. The big complaint in the memos and the phone calls to the set indicated that their initial fears about the film's being too dark and terrifying (and so contrary to the carefully cultivated Disney family image) were very much alive. Consequently, what was shaping up as a stereotype-breaking performance by Hawn, in which, according to those close to the production, she was displaying believable levels of fear, anger, and emotional torment, was being diluted. "First they changed the name of the film from *The Mrs.* to *Deceived.* Then they began asking for script changes." according to director Harris.

Consequently Hawn was spending a lot of late nights on the phone, arguing with Disney executives in an attempt to save the edgier elements of the film that were slowly but surely being compromised into a highly predictable and stilted film.

Hawn came off *Deceived* with mixed feelings. She felt good about parts of the movie and less than good about others. She felt the final fate of *Deceived* would be in the hands of the director, and of course, despite the best efforts of Disney, for whom she was having not such positive feelings, she would have her input. But all she could think of at the moment was quiet time with her family.

Russell, coming off *Backdraft,* was also in need of a little R & R. In the summer of 1991, they decided they needed to go where the phones would never ring and chose to take a leisurely family bike trip through Europe. As they were making preparations for the trip, Goldie took a last look at business matters and at a script called *HouseSitter.*

It looked like a relatively entertaining project. That Steve Martin was rumored to be attached piqued her interest. She made the appropriate calls and found that the project was still in limbo and would be for quite a while. Goldie filed *HouseSitter* away for future reference and packed her bags.

By all accounts the bike holiday through Europe, particularly Paris and Brittany, was a joy. Goldie, Kurt, and the children would spend their days on the gently sloping roads, passing through quaint villages and stopping when they felt like it to enjoy a leisurely lunch or shop and staying at various charming hotels and inns. When a telephone did occasionally ring in their presence, it was a safe bet that it wasn't for Goldie or Kurt.

But the couple did sometimes check their messages. Goldie shrugged her shoulders when she discovered that Meg Ryan had accepted the role in *HouseSitter*. Near the end of their vacation, she received an unexpected call from the States. It was her agent. Meg Ryan had backed out of *HouseSitter*, claiming that the character "lacked motivation." Was she still interested? She was. And Disney, good as their word, let her run across town to another studio to do it.

The reason Goldie was willing to cut her vacation short was that *HouseSitter* was not, to her way of thinking, a typical comedy. This tale of a New England architect who runs afoul of a flighty nonconformist with a penchant for lies was a hybrid of sorts. On one page, Goldie saw a romantic comedy; on another, a straightforward laugh fest, on yet another, a farce of the broadest kind. With director Frank Oz at the helm and Steve Martin now totally commited to the project, she saw something potentially special in the film.

HouseSitter proved to be a good fit. The constant change of pace forced Goldie to keep shifting gears from wide-eyed innocent to wacked-out logical thinker and all emotional points in between. With his portrayal of the constantly perplexed and worrisome opposite, Martin was the perfect foil and the film benefited from the fact that Oz, despite a rock-solid script, left plenty of room to improvise.

Meanwhile, the Hawn-Russell relationship was closing in on the seven-year mark and the couple appeared more in love than ever. As always, there continued to be questions about when they were going to make their union legal. They were patient in mouthing the same comments about their love being more important than marriage.

Privately, the subject of marriage was often the topic of much laughter. "We tease each other about marriage a lot," Hawn said. "In fact, Kurt called me on the phone the other night and said, 'Marry me and take me away from all this.'"

Russell continued to prove how committed he was by gathering Goldie and the children in their bedroom for a celebration of seven years of their love. Once again, Kurt presented Goldie with a diamond-encrusted "common law" ring. They were quite happy with the way things were, but they had begun to discuss the effect their relationship had had and would have on their children.

"Once in a while," recalled Goldie, "the kids would harp on it. It's not something we think about every day, but when the kids make a comment, we do."

And so, around the time she was making *HouseSitter,* Goldie and Kurt decided to put the question of marriage to a vote. They gathered Oliver, Kate, Boston, and Wyatt together, and the family took a vote on whether their parents should marry. The children unanimously turned their thumbs down.

Deceived and *Backdraft* came out in 1991, within a couple of months of each other. Goldie was happy that Kurt's big action release received decent reviews and did solid box office. Russell did his best to help Goldie through the less positive reception accorded *Deceived.* Reviewers jumped on the fact that the thrills were not that thrilling and that Hawn's performance, while good, was derivative of those of other actresses in distress films and made the movie all the more predictable. *Deceived* would do only passable business and quickly left theaters.

Disney was disappointed that their first project with Hawn had not been a success. In closed-door meetings, executives expressed concern that Hawn had been perhaps too anxious to exercise her option to work for another studio. Disney began working overtime, separately and in conjunction with Hawn, to develop another project for her under the Disney banner. A romantic comedy called *Zippers and Skirts,* which allegedly had the ear of Michael Douglas, was floated as a possible Goldie vehicle. So was a comedy called *Family Values.*

On her own, Goldie was continuing to run up against a wall in an attempt to get *Last Wish* and *Babe West* off the ground. She was also working closely with Warner Bros. to develop a big-budget remake of *Auntie Mame*. At that point two other scripts struck her fancy: one a special effects-fantasy called *Death Becomes Her,* the other a drama that sparked her interest, *Crisscross.*

Crisscross told the very real world story of a single mother who supports herself and her twelve-year-old son by waitressing during the day and, unbeknownst to her son, stripping at night. When the son accidentally discovers her night work, he begins to sell drugs in an attempt to get his mother to give up her stripping job. Adding to their emotional turmoil, the mother attempts to reconcile with the father of her son, a disgraced Vietnam vet who has walked out on them. *Crisscross* struck a very personal chord. She felt the pain of the story and saw the black comedy as well.

"It's about what we do to our children," Hawn said in touting the quality of the script. "We're living in a world where people get married two and three times and have to learn to get along in extended families. Sometimes they do, sometimes they don't, but the pity of it all is what we end up doing to the kids. I saw it as a love story about a mother and son who don't always do what's right. That's the reason for this movie."

Her passion for *Crisscross* was so strong that she insisted on producing as well as starring in it. Goldie once again became the woman in power as she began pulling all the creative and technical elements together. Warner Bros. knew that *Crisscross* was a relatively small movie. But they also sensed, as did Goldie, that it contained an all-important message and held the potential for some possible acting nods when Oscar time rolled around.

Once again Hawn went the unorthodox route in casting and choosing a director. She went primarily with proven character actors and in the case of director Chris Menges, a relative unknown whose previous film, *A World Apart,* addressed heavy political and social issues through the eyes of a child whose age was close to that of the child in *Crisscross.* Goldie was encouraged.

But an unexpected problem surfaced for *Crisscross.* Owing to a recent change in the U.S. visa policy, a number of British members of the *Crisscross* crew, including the cinematographer, editor, and art director, were denied work visas. In her producer's role, Hawn spent a number of days unsuccessfully fighting the red tape before finally giving in and bravely announcing that "the shake-up will not disrupt the production in the least." Once filming started, she put the problems behind her and found solace and salvation in her very personalized approach to the role.

Those on the set of *Crisscross* were aware of Goldie's history and how she might be dredging up both the negative and positive in it for this role. Her scenes with the child often had crew members biting their lips at the range of emotion they were seeing. The scenes between Goldie and the actor playing her ex-husband bristled with a fiery tension that obviously had its origin in her still-negative feelings toward Bill Hudson. The actress also made the most of the fleeting scenes of her character stripping in the bar. Goldie was drawing on her days as a New York go-go dancer to project the hardened, disinterested, frosty attitude of a person who was doing this under silent protest.

Hawn was joyous as *Crisscross* neared completion, confident that she was giving her strongest dramatic performance to date. And she was looking forward to jumping right into another test, the special-effects heavy comedy *Death Becomes Her,* opposite her good buddy Meryl Streep.

Death Becomes Her, a comic send-up of the pursuit of youth and immortality, focused on Helen Sharp, a mousy woman who balloons to four hundred pounds when her plastic surgeon boyfriend, Ernest Menville, is stolen by tacky cabaret star Madeline Ashton. The women discover a magic potion that not only shaves years, wrinkles, and pounds off their bodies but gives them an insatiable urge for revenge.

Goldie loved the script. Its highlights included a scene in which Madeline appears with her head facing one way and her body the other as well as a sequence in which Madeline fires a shotgun at Helen, blowing a very large and exaggerated hole out of her middle. She had never experienced the process of prosthetic special effects firsthand (although Kurt would often regale her with makeup stories on his films *Escape From New York, The Thing* and *Big Trouble in Little China*) and was excited at the prospect. She was also eager to work with Streep for the first time. The choice of Bruce Willis for the male lead ended a protracted undertaking after Kevin Kline dropped out of the role and negotiations with Jeff Bridges and Nick Nolte broke down.

Director Robert Zemeckis was no stranger to this kind of madness, having effectively pushed special effects into the twenty-first century with *Who Framed Roger Rabbit?* He knew from the beginning that Hawn was perfect for the role of Helen (even though Goldie made a big run at playing Madeline), and he had no qualms about her ability to handle *Death Becomes Her*'s particular brand of humor. "Goldie is an old pro and incredibly talented," Zemeckis said. "Doing this kind of stuff is like a second sense to her. I also liked the idea of casting Goldie against how she's been traditionally cast. I know Goldie has never been seen as a psycho murderess."

What Goldie had not counted on was having to do a lot of chair time in a special-effects shop prior to the start of filming, having molds taken of her face and body for the four hundred-pound fat suit. Goldie was a trooper as the mold-making process buried her face, arms, and body under icky compounds.

"The suit was sculpted out of clay," recalled Zemeckis of Goldie's getup. "The finished suit was more like a space suit that she would step into."

Goldie's good spirits extended into the first day of filming. With good friend Streep sitting nearby, the makeup trailer on *Death Becomes Her* was rocking with laughter, gossip, and talk of kids (in particular, Streep's new baby) that made the daily four-hour process by which Goldie was transformed into fat Helen much more bearable.

In fact, her willingness to bend and twist herself to accommodate the blueprint of the film's computer-effects technology made her a favorite with behind-the-scenes people, who all had their stories about temperamental artists. When it came time for the sequence in which the shotgun blast puts a Frisbee-sized hole in Helen's middle, Goldie would stand still for long periods of time as the technical people positioned her body and face to line up the effects shot that would be sent back to the lab for computer enhancement. For a scene near the end of the film in which Helen and Madeline's bodies fall down the stairs and shatter, leaving only the talking heads, Zemeckis had Goldie "act out her lines hanging upside down in a harness" so that a clean computer graft of her head could be taken."

Goldie completed *Death Becomes Her* early in 1992 and returned to the Aspen homestead for a stretch of family time. She shook off the mantle of professional woman and became wife and mother, helping Oliver with his homework, shuttling Kate back and forth to dance lessons, and cooking up big Sunday dinners that would often include the bounty of Kurt's recent hunting trip and just as often turn into mammoth affairs, with their friends and the friends of their children, who were always welcome.

Workwise Goldie was at a standstill due to a large extent her stubborn decree that she was looking for something more substantial. Disney was still hustling to get another Goldie project going but, three years into the deal, was coming up empty.

Goldie was not in any hurry. Owing to the vagaries of studio release schedules, she now had the luxury of three pictures in the can that would be coming out over a three-month period during the summer. Goldie was more than willing to kick back and relax....

When tragedy struck.

12

Why Am I Doing This?

GOLDIE HAWN KNEW HER MOTHER WAS SLOWING DOWN.

Laura Hawn, well into her seventh decade, was moving slower these days and would regularly have to stop to rest. When she would visit the Aspen compound, she would sometimes complain of shortness of breath. Goldie assumed that the problem was the result of being in a higher altitude.

How sick Laura Hawn actually was became horrifyingly clear in 1992 when she had a heart attack. Goldie was at her mother's side throughout her hospital stay, fighting back the memories of the all-night vigils that had ended with the death of her father and hoping against hope that the scenario was not going to be played out again. The doctors put Laura Hawn through the expected battery of tests, and while it was finally determined that Goldie's mother could go home, the tests also confirmed that she had heart disease and that it was only a matter of time.

As she checked her mother out of the hospital, Goldie made the decision to put her career on hold so that she could be with her mother in her last days. "When elephants are dying, the rest of the herd gather around and support them," said Hawn of her decision. "I decided to do that for my mom."

Goldie, Kurt, and the children closed up their Aspen residence and moved back to Los Angeles. Goldie moved her mother into the Pacific Palisades home and took her business phone off the hook.

Goldie's world grew more withdrawn and centered totally on the life and needs of her mother. A good day was measured by how often her mother was pain-free and could laugh and smile. A bad day was emotionally draining as Goldie and her family dealt with Laura's pain and the days when she was too weak to get out of bed.

When Laura was up to it, recalled Hawn in looking back on those days, Goldie would sit with her in the living room for hours, entertaining her with songs, stories, and jokes that would have the house echoing with the best kind of laughter. At a time when her mother's impending death should have been a constant strain, Goldie was finding a strange kind of peace in being an active participant in her mother's last days.

"Having my mother live with me was a joy," she said of those final months. "I was able to take care of her, and the children had an opportunity to live with their grandmother, which I felt was very important."

She was up-front, especially with the two older children, in explaining that their grandmother had been sick and that's why she was staying with them for a while. The question would inevitably arise from Oliver or Kate as to whether their grandmother was going to die. Goldie was torn during those moments, wondering how much she should tell them and how much they would understand. Finally, she would do her best to explain that everybody died eventually and that, hopefully, their grandmother would be around for a long time.

The presummer release of *Crisscross* brought a momentary break from the vigil. Hawn did very little press for the film, not wanting to deal with the inevitable questions about her real-life crisis.

The reviews were mixed. Some critics applauded the low-key nature of the film while others deplored the approach as being sluggish. Reviewers were also quick to dismiss the voice-overs as distracting and excessive. Goldie was happy to receive generally good notices for her serious acting turn, but she barely blinked an eye as *Crisscross* failed to attract even the hard-core Goldie audience and soon disappeared from theaters.

In the wake of *Crisscross*'s failure to light up the box office, Goldie had become extremely unhappy with the strain of producing and the frustration of seeing her efforts translate into lackluster results. She quietly dissolved the Movie Company but maintained a good relationship with Sylbert and an agreement to produce together again at some point in the future. When that would be, she could not say for sure.

For the time being, she had other, more important things on her mind.

Goldie's days with her mother turned into a lot of small moments: reliving childhood memories, telling risqué jokes that would dissolve them both into fits of laughter, enjoying the daily comings and goings of the children, whose most mundane tales of school and play took on major importance in the mind of Laura Hawn.

Midsummer saw the release of *HouseSitter*. Despite the high hopes for the Hawn-Martin pairing, the critics, while conceding that the film had quite a few comedic moments, noted that it did not have much of a script and that the story was ultimately aimless and not compelling. The public went to see *HouseSitter*, but not in great numbers. According to the film pundits, Goldie had a core audience that would go see her in anything, but she was unable to expand beyond that group in the way she had with *Private Benjamin*.

Goldie paid only scant attention to this latest setback and turned to her mother as only a devoted daughter would. The Hawn family celebrated a rather quiet Fourth of July: A gathering of family and friends watched fireworks, ate a big homestyle meal and simply rejoiced in the concept of family. The celebration had added significance. While Laura Hawn's spirits remained upbeat, her condition was deteriorating steadily. But while Laura Hawn was still vital, Goldie and her family insisted on celebrating her life in the best possible way—with laughs, hugs, and tears.

Death Becomes Her hit theaters in late July, and the results were encouraging. While many critics stated that the impressive special effects were the sole reason for seeing the film, an equal number gave it points for its engaging streak of black comedy and the fact that Hawn, Streep, and Willis held up quite well in the face of the aforementioned FX elements. *Death Becomes Her* drew a massive audience response and went on to be an even bigger box-office success than Hawn's last hit, *Bird on a Wire*. Goldie was encouraged.

The holiday season was a joyous time, with a mix of Christmas and Hanukkah symbolism and a family gathering of classic proportions. The smile on Laura Hawn's face as the children raced around the house and handed her gifts was just the holiday Goldie needed.

Goldie was constantly at her mother's side during the early part of 1993. *Auntie Mame* and *Family Values* were continuing in development as possible vehicles for her but were going nowhere, due in large part to Goldie's refusal to commit to anything that might take her away from her mother. She would occasionally look at a script but could not muster up much enthusiasm or a strong opinion on anything.

As spring gave way to summer, there was a noticeable decline in Laura's condition and Goldie sensed that the end was near. Her mother hung on through the summer and most of the fall. Then it was finally over. Laura Hawn died of a heart attack on November 27, 1993. Goldie was crushed.

"When my mother was alive, I was a daughter first and everything else second," she said after her mother's death. "That's what made her death so painful. My mother was a big part of my life and a big reason why I did what I did. I've always derived a lot of energy from being a good daughter. There was a lot of devotion on my part for what she did for me and how she encouraged me. I just couldn't wait to share all the good things that were happening to me with her. When she was gone, I suddenly thought, Why am I doing all this? For whom? Losing my mom was really hard on me. I remember going to the Academy Awards shortly after she died and thinking, Well I'm all dressed up, and my mother won't see me."

By early 1994, the consensus was that Hawn had gone through

her period of grieving and would be thinking about getting on with her life. But Goldie continued in a somber, sad, reflective mood, paying only lip service to the most necessary of business obligations. The last thing on Goldie Hawn's mind was her next picture, or her career.

"After my mom died, I really did not want to go back to work. In a large sense I turned a page in my life when my mother passed on. I realized that all the things I had been doing were simply not enough. My production company was not working the way I wanted it to, and my agents were not working the way I wanted them to."

Goldie spent much of 1994 in relative seclusion in her Aspen home. For a time there was no news to report regarding her future. When Goldie finally had something to say, the news was a bombshell of some proportion. She announced that she would be restructuring her production company and that she would be changing agents. None of this was done with any grand plan in mind, and one can only speculate that it was part of Goldie's plan of material and emotional housecleaning.

It was a drastic and, by Hollywood standards, totally unexpected decision. Hollywood wags began putting various spins on it. Some saw it, rightly, as a reaction to the death of her mother. The more cynical in town pointed to her recent film disasters and the failure of Disney to make anything out of their much-publicized deal with her as the reason for her drastic attempt at restarting a flagging career.

Goldie felt the time was simply right for a change.

"It was simply time to take control of my life," she said. "My mom used to say 'Goldie, you've got to do it yourself and stop depending on other people.' My mother's death was a big passage for me."

The new chapter in Goldie Hawn's life still did not include much of an emphasis on acting matters. Yes, she was reading scripts. But Hawn was primarily using the occasion of her mother's death to immerse herself in Indian and European spiritual philosophies, especially as they pertained to the concepts of life and death. She did a lot of traveling and much of what she considered "spiritual work." She made a number of trips to India, spent a lot of time with Kurt and the children, and was seemingly relieved at the prospect of taking life a bit easier and charting a more balanced course through her life and work.

It was during the early stages of her extended period away from show business that Goldie came to an important decision regarding her past and her future. In a sense, she was admitting defeat by justifying her decision to not actively fight the world's long-standing perception of her as the laugh queen.

"The reality is that I've never been taken seriously," she conceded. "Even after the success of *Private Benjamin*, I was taken seriously in a business sense, but even at that point everyone still wanted to see me in a certain way. What I've learned is that people need to see in me what they want to see. Even when I've done a drama like *The Sugarland Express* or *The Girl From Petrovka* I would still get comments like 'When are you going to do your drama?' So I finally realized that being taken seriously is only a small part of it and that making people laugh and be happy can be serious in a whole different way."

Goldie Hawn would not work again for another two years. She was dealing with much deeper concerns than box office and stardom. "I was coming to grips with death," reflected Goldie, "and what it was all about."

13

How Does It Feel
to Turn Fifty?

GOLDIE HAWN EMERGED FROM THE ANTIQUES SHOP JUST IN TIME
to watch a young crook ride off down the street on her bicycle. In
another life, Goldie would have run back into the store, called the
police, and hoped for the best. But that was not the person Goldie
Hawn was in 1994.

She dropped her purchases and raced down the street after the
bike thief, her dancer's body working overtime as she screamed at
him. After chasing the thief for more than two hundred yards,
Goldie caught up with the him. She got right in his face, screaming
obscenities. With a mighty shove, the bike thief went flying off the
bike and hit the ground. He looked up in amazement. Goldie was
standing over him, breathing hard, an angry scowl on her face. If
looks could kill, the bike thief's life was about to be over. He got up
and ran off as Hawn, picking up the bike, continued to scream at
him.

This one crime-fighting adventure was about as exciting as
things got during Goldie's four years away from the business. And
that was fine with her. Being the car-pool mom for Wyatt and his
classmates and dealing with the teenage angst of Oliver and Kate

were motherly challenges more mundane than piloting the fortunes of a major motion picture, but to Goldie at that point in her life they were more important than anything she could conceive of doing professionally.

So was traveling, either alone or with Kurt or sister Patti to faraway places. Her hiatus had once again coincided with an increase in Kurt's workload, and so she would often travel to the locations of such films as *Captain Ron* and *Tombstone* to be with him. The couple also expanded their residential empire when they discovered the beautiful Muskoka cottage country of Ontario, Canada, purchased a parcel of land on the shores of Lake Rousseau, and began building what they described as "a summer residence."

While Goldie was taking a well-deserved vacation, Hollywood was changing. Women, thanks in no small part to the groundbreaking work done by Hawn, were gaining increasingly more power in front of and behind the camera. Actresses like Julia Roberts and Demi Moore were beginning to command the same kind of payday as their male counterparts. And to the world at large Goldie Hawn was being left in the dust.

Goldie had not been totally out of touch with Hollywood. After a long period of inactivity, her production company, Cherry Alley, had executive-produced the Julia Roberts–Dennis Quaid comedy *Something to Talk About* (1996). While Hawn was given the title of executive producer, her old partner, Anthea Sylbert, did most of the trench work. The film, about the funny side of two-timing, received mixed reviews and did so-so business upon its release.

During this period, Goldie limited her appearances to television. When Chevy Chase landed what would be a short-lived late-night talk show in 1994, Goldie agreed to guest on the first show. It was just the kind of no-brainer situation that Goldie felt comfortable with. Chase fired softball questions, and the pair cracked one-liners as they laughed it up over old times.

That same year, Goldie returned to her roots when she joined in the good times that were *Rowan And Martin's Laugh-In 25th Anniversary Special.* The reunion TV special was a bittersweet experience for Goldie. It was the first time she had seen many of the

Laugh-In cast members since she had left the show, and so there was the expected sharing of memories and career and personal updates. Sadly, what the reunion showed was that for many of the cast members, *Laugh-In* had been the high point of their careers, and while most of them continued to make a living in entertainment, none had approached the level of stardom that Goldie had. She dismissed the press questions of success and failure by saying that she had only been lucky.

In the meantime, the rumor line was ripe with reports that Goldie had gotten out of the business for good. The reports further suggested that she had always been a one-note performer and, in closing in on age fifty, had run out the rope of ditzy, dumb-blond parts. Rather than get upset, Goldie laughed off the reports.

"Someone asked me recently, 'Now that you're older, don't you wish you could play the ingenue just one more time?'" She responded to the question of aging gracefully. "And I said, 'Are you nuts?' I love this stage of my life. Fifty is just a number for me. Turning fifty was just amazing. It was so cool!"

Goldie had not come by this simple logic overnight. She readily acknowledged, as far back as *Bird on a Wire,* that playing young and adorable was becoming uncomfortable and, more importantly, unbelievable in her own eyes. But she had kept at it and, as recently as 1992's *HouseSitter,* had made a token attempt at keeping the old Goldie alive. But Goldie knew that it would be ludicrous and an embarrassment to try to resurrect an image that was at least fifteen years behind the reality of her life.

Out of the public eye, Hawn was actively preparing for the next phase of her life. While her production company was actively involved in a number of non-Goldie projects, she was consulting with writers, and reading scripts, and indulging herself in projects like the PBS documentary *The Elephants of India.* The project, part of the educational channel's acclaimed *In the Wild* series, appealed to Goldie for a number of reasons. There was her love of animals, especially elephants, and, of course, there was her long-held affection for all things relating to India. And so, in May 1995, she ventured into the wild jungles of India to tell the tale of the life and times of a particular elephant herd.

The Elephants of India was not a sugar-coated look at wildlife. Goldie was definitely roughing it as she led the camera crew and viewers through an odyssey that explored elephant society and what had become of a particular herd's members over the years. Goldie was enthusiastic in recalling the experience. "It was exciting, but I was sometimes frightened to death. But if you look into the eyes of an elephant, they're the kindest eyes you've ever seen."

In the midst of being a mother, wife, and producer, Goldie paused to look back on her childhood years. Something in that swirl of memories jumped out at her. She sat down and started to write *Duck and Cover*, a story of a young girl coming of age in Washington, D.C., in the shadow of the atomic bomb, a story that had its origins in Goldie's youth. As she wrote, Goldie still shuddered at the memory of her elementary school days when her class would be led into the visual-aids room and subjected to grainy black-and-white "educational" films portraying children being rocked out of their daily activities by the sudden flash of light that signaled an atomic-bomb attack.

"This story was my story," said Goldie of the inspiration for *Duck and Cover*. "I would run home and ask my mom over and over again: 'Please explain why the Russians aren't going to bomb us.' I wouldn't go to school when I knew there would be an air-raid test because it frightened me so much on such a deep level. When I was twelve, my girlfriend and I had heard that oilcloth would protect us from radiation. So every time we would hear the air raid siren, we would run down into the basement of my house, cover ourselves in oilcloth, and scream that we were going to die. It made me aware, for the first time, that I was mortal and that I was going to die. I didn't think I was going to live to kiss a boy, fall in love, or learn to drive."

She threw herself into writing the story. It was something personal, a concept that challenged the serenity of her childhood and continued to occupy the dark passages of her memories. The words flowed out of her, as did the feeling that the message was important.

"Nobody had ever told this story," she said. "Nobody ever told us what happened to those young men and women who grew up in the cold war."

Six months after Goldie finished writing *Duck and Cover*, a script came over the transom that knocked her socks off. It was called *Hope*.

Hope, written by Kerry Kennedy, told the story of a young girl coming of age in the South in 1962 and having to confront family issues, racism, and cold-war fears. Goldie read the script in stunned silence. "I didn't believe it!," she recalled. "For the first time, I found something that I understood so deeply."

Hawn was so touched by *Hope* that she immediately decided that the only way this story would survive intact in the Hollywood system was if she were there every step of the way. The only way *Hope* would be successfully made was if she directed it.

Directing was not a brand-new notion for Goldie. The thought had been in her mind for years, even before she considered producing. Subconsciously, she had been preparing for the role for years. Goldie had always been curious about what occurred on the other side of the camera and would often spend her off time looking over directors' shoulders, mentally figuring out how they made the magic. During the last year of his life, Goldie's father had regularly questioned her about when she was going to direct. Goldie would brush the idea aside, saying that it would take even more time away from her children than her career was already doing.

"When I first considered directing, years ago, my children were little, and I was afraid it would take me away from them and would make me preoccupied," she said. "I was afraid I would not be able to give love to them if they came to the set. So I kept saying, 'Not now, not now. Maybe when I get older.'"

But with two teenagers and one child fast approaching the preteen stage, Goldie reasoned that the time was right to reemerge into the working world as a director at the helm of *Hope*. "At the time, I had not been working in a long time, and I thought this would be a great transition to make."

Goldie put the word out that she was attached to *Hope* but that this package deal was contingent on her directing rather than starring in it. The initial reaction was mixed. Studio executives were glad that Goldie was back and were quick to offer up suggestions for old-Goldie types of scripts. But they were not necessarily willing to let their money ride on Hawn's first-ever directing job. The TNT Cable Television Network, however, had had experience giving star actors their maiden directing jobs (Tommy Lee Jones, for one) and almost immediately said yes to Hawn.

Goldie enthusiastically jumped into the early stages of preproduction on *Hope*. It was at this point that two other scripts landed on her desk. *Everybody Says I Love You* and *The First Wives' Club* had pedigrees that brought her plans for directing to a grinding halt.

Everyone Says I Love You, a Woody Allen project, immediately caught Goldie's eye. And typical of the notoriously quirky filmmaker, it was shrouded in mystery. What was known was that the film would focus in a tragicomic way on the breakup of relationships and how former partners interact. What came as a complete surprise to Hawn was that Allen, rather than going with an ensemble of more cerebral actors, as he usually did, was actively seeking out the likes of Julia Roberts, Edward Norton, and Drew Barrymore to fill out the cast. Goldie was shocked that Allen would come looking for her.

"I had seen her [Hawn] years ago in one of those Broadway plays [*Butterflies Are Free*] that had been made into a movie and had seen her in the one with Bergman [*Cactus Flower*]," recalled Allen of his decision to recruit Hawn. "I thought she was always amusing and had always wanted to work with her."

The First Wives' Club also proved too good to be true. It was a classic 1990s story of revenge. Three old friends get together at the funeral of a friend who killed herself after her husband dumped her for another woman. The three mourners, who have, likewise been dumped, band together to get even with their husbands.

It was comedy in the broadest sense—something that Goldie had done many times before. But she liked the idea that Bette Midler and Diane Keaton, like Goldie, right at age fifty, were also attached. More important was that *The First Wives' Club* was telling a story

173

that hit very close to home. Goldie liked the anger and the male bashing inherent in the tale and felt that the characters, in a comic sense, rang true.

Goldie was faced with the best and worst of decisions. If she took the film offers, she would have to relinquish all rights to *Hope*. After much thought the lure of the acting roles proved too hard to resist. "I had to give it away," said Hawn of *Hope*. "The TNT people were very nice about it. They said they would go ahead and hire somebody else to direct."

Everybody Says I Love You, filmed in New York, Paris, and Venice, turned out to be one wild ride. And one that, by design, continued to be shrouded in mystery. Allen had waited until two weeks before the production began before telling his cast of largely nonsinging and dancing stars that they were involved in a musical. Goldie laughed at the surprise. A lot of the others panicked, and Allen had to do a super selling job to convince them that the best they could do would be fine. The filmmaker, for the sake of spontaneity, continued to keep his actors in the dark, giving them only basic-story scripts and necessary dialogue pages the night before filming.

Goldie Hawn presented a particular challenge to the film's bizarre singing and dancing numbers that populated the film. "I knew Goldie as a very funny actress," Allen recalled. "But I had never met her before. So when we started to film the singing and dancing, I discovered that she was a professional."

An immediate, good-natured conference took place. "I was asked to rein in my voice so as not to upstage the less experienced singers," said Goldie. "Even when we got into the recording studio, after the filming, Woody would be flipping out and saying, 'Could you please sing less?'"

However, Goldie's experience with dance was definitely a plus once the *Everybody Says I Love You* production moved to Paris, where some of the more complex singing and dancing numbers were to take place. During the filming in Paris, Allen was expressing some concern about how a showstopping dance number, to be filmed along the River Siene, was going to come off. As it turned out, it was Allen who was pressed to learn the elements. Hawn instinctively knew where each step had to be. "We just walked through it a couple of times," Allen remembered. "All we had to do was figure out where to put the cameras and the lights. The scene itself came together fairly easy."

Goldie completed *Everybody Says I Love You* and returned home, preparing to jump right into *The First Wives' Club*. However, she was suddenly having second thoughts about doing the film. She had missed her family and was not looking forward to another extended stay apart from them. Her initial enthusiasm for the film had also begun to wane. She was suddenly uncomfortable with the male-bashing nature of the script and felt that the story was just too angry in tone. And finally, given her history of failed marriages, she felt that playing this character would strike too close to home.

Paul Rudnick, one of the writers who worked on *The First Wives' Club* script, felt he knew where Goldie was coming from. "I think that Goldie was aware that the audience might identify her with the character she plays," he speculated. "She knew the movie was going to be played for laughs, but that kind of thing can be touchy. You know how it is when a gorgeous blond turns fifty."

All Goldie knew was that the prospect of doing *The First Wives' Club* suddenly had her scared to death. "I was really wondering how I was going to get out of doing this movie."

Paramount Studios honcho Sherry Lansing, upon hearing of Goldie's sudden indecision about the film, had worries of her own. Lansing feared that if Hawn quit the film, it would open the floodgates for others to leave the project as well. She did not want to play hardball with Hawn. But she felt she had no choice.

A meeting was set up between the two women. There was obvious tension in the air as they laid their cards on the table. Lansing patiently outlined the film's intent, a comic send-up of relationships aimed at the baby-boomer generation that was meant to be fun while making some potent statements about the fragile nature of relationships in the 1990s. She listened intently as Hawn expressed her own personal concerns about the project. Lansing, in response, made it plain that a lawsuit might be forthcoming if Goldie walked out on the film.

Sitting on the sidelines as Lansing and Hawn battled it out was *The First Wives' Club* director Hugh Wilson, who saw the threat of a lawsuit as a bad sign. "I remember thinking, 'Oh, great! Some big star is going to be coming in here mad as hell! This could be real bad.'"

The idea of having to once again spend time in court finally won out over Hawn's reservations, about the film and so she reluctantly reported to *The First Wives' Club* set on the first day of filming. Wilson was standing at a far corner of the set when Goldie walked in. He had freely admitted in preproduction remarks that he was initially intimidated at the prospect of directing the three superstar women. It did not add to his confidence level that Goldie was doing the film grudgingly. In an attempt to break the ice as well as gauge her feelings, he walked over to Goldie and whispered in her ear, "You couldn't dodge the bullet, could you?" Goldie smiled and said, "Nah, honey. Here I am. Let's go for it."

Putting the best possible face on an uncomfortable situation, Hawn squared her shoulders on that first day and soon found herself having fun. To a large extent, the about-face can be attributed to the instant rapport she established with her costars Midler and Keaton. She instantly recognized that they were very much like her. Midler was outrageous and brash, as Goldie could often be, while in Keaton's more laid back approach to things, Goldie saw herself in her more reflective moods. An instant bond formed among the three leading ladies.

Keaton laughingly recalled how it was not uncommon for Hawn and Midler to spontaneously erupt into song. There was also the day when director Wilson, attempting to get his actresses back to the set, watched in amusement as the trio began a mock fight in which Midler had Hawn in a headlock and Keaton was attempting to gouge out Midler's eyes with a teasing comb.

Midler, in commenting on the scene, said, "It's a lot of fun working with women. With women, you can let your hair down, and the fur flies."

Hawn agreed. "Working with Kurt aside, this really is the most

176

fun I've ever had on a movie. There's no tension. The ego thing is out the window. There's been no competition."

The First Wives' Club had turned into what one crew member described as "a pajama party." Hawn, as the production progressed, had come to grips with the issues that had bothered her, and they had pretty much evaporated. In fact, Goldie had become so comfortable with the material, she was regularly buttonholing screenwriter Rudnick, filling his ear with real-life tales of her two divorces in an attempt to help him flesh out her character.

"She had a lot of experience in that area," recalled the film's producer Scott Rudin, "and she wanted to bring it to the movie."

Goldie's continued good spirits on the set became a highlight for her fellow workers. Director Wilson said seeing Goldie every day "was like the sun coming out." Keaton used the sun reference in explaining how "this golden haze would appear around her" when she was in her makeup chair each morning.

"And the most amazing thing about her is you don't see her working," continued Keaton. "With her it just happens."

Goldie, it was reported, adopted a totally different persona when dealing with the film's younger, less experienced actors. She was always available when John Stewart had a question or appeared unsure of how to play a scene. She was particularly protective of Elizabeth Berkley, who had just come off a critical beating in *Showgirls* and would occasionally appear vulnerable and lost. "I guess it was because I was missing my own children," said Hawn of the den mother in her.

Not that *The First Wives' Club* was totally stress-free. Midler, at one point in the production, admitted that things were not perfect. "It's been a lot of fun," she said, "but it hasn't been a love fest." And all three women were occasionally heard to bitch about too many unnecessary takes.

Her spirits buoyed by weekend trips home to be with Kurt and the children, Goldie remained upbeat even to the point of addressing the age question in both her character and in real life. "Older?" she said during an on set interview. "We are older."

Hawn completed *The First Wives' Club* in a positive state of mind, confident that her work in that film and *Everybody Says I Love* You would be a strong indication to Hollywood that she was definitely back. Her spirits soared during the final few months of 1996 when she received a telephone call from TNT. The person they had hired to direct *Hope* had backed out of the project "for personal reasons," and the producers wanted to know if she was still interested in directing the film.

Goldie's joy at a second chance was once again tempered by the fact that directing her first film would be an all-consuming job that would cut down on her time with her family. She could not do it with a clear conscience unless she had her family's blessing.

So she called another of those Hawn-Russell family meetings and explained how she would be spending the entire summer on location in Texas and that directing *Hope* would interfere with their normal vacation time. Goldie held her breath as an informal vote was taken. Her mind was already made up. Now all she needed was validation from her family.

"And you know what?" related an excited Hawn. "Everyone gave me their blessing. My daughter, Kate, said she was glad I was going to direct this film because she had seen how much it meant to me and how disappointed I had been when I had to give it up."

Typically, Russell was succinct in his support. "You know, honey, I think it's time."

14

Hope

GOLDIE ROLLED UP HER SLEEVES AND JUMPED RIGHT INTO preproduction on *Hope* in Los Angeles. A lot of what she was doing was not all that unfamiliar to her. As a producer she had waded through writer's conferences, attended long hours of casting sessions, and checked the credentials of directors until her eyes were crossed. She had scouted out locations, checked equipment companies for the lowest bids and burned the midnight oil contending with the often paranoid calls from insecure studio heads.

But *Hope* was different. She would be dealing with hundreds of people on a far-flung location. Her decision would be the final one. Thus, as *Hope* began to take shape, there were long days and frustrating nights when answers seemed impossible to find. But find them Goldie did.

In her most optimistic of moments, Goldie had envisioned *Hope* as a small theatrical release. But the reality of the industry, in which high concept often takes precedence over small and intimate in the battle for the nation's movie screens, finally hit home and Hawn realized that the best chance for *Hope* was on the small screen. And the reality of a movie for television meant that Goldie would have to contend with a meager twenty-eight-day shooting schedule and a budget that was one-tenth that of even a modest-budget theatrical film. Opinion on whether Goldie could pull it off or was getting in over her head under these constraints was divided. Goldie felt she could handle the limitations.

"I had a lot to think about. I had been warned that I would probably be answering about six hundred questions a day and that it would be very difficult. But my feeling was that I had dealt with my family and supervised the remodeling of a house while hanging twenty stories above the street making *Bird on a Wire*. So I was sure I could make this movie."

She was more than a bit skittish, however, about how all those years projecting a dumb-blond image would wash with the authoritarian figure she would have to be on the set of *Hope*, with its traditionally rough-and-tumble, blue-collar, and decidedly male crew.

"My feeling was that if I came up against this friction with someone or this lack of communication, I would have to pull that person aside and explain to them that 'unfortunately, this is where I am right now, and this is where you are,'" said Hawn of those early concerns. "So if we don't have a line of communication, one of us is going to have to go."

Goldie need not have feared how rough union crews would react to her. Technical people were anxious to sign on to the film and admitted, money aside, that there was a certain amount of curiosity on their part as to how Goldie as director would fare. But most seemed confident that she could handle it.

Nevertheless, doubts about her ability to make the transition from actor to director continued to nag at her as she prepared to make *Hope*. Goldie had always projected a softer, more spiritual, non-aggressive approach in her dealings with people, preferring to make her points with logic rather than emotion. And it was that spiritual awareness of just what made her tick that was causing her second thoughts. "I was concerned, right from the start, how this job might change me. That was the one thing I never wanted to have happen."

Everybody Says I Love You opened in a few showcase theaters in early fall 1996. The reviews were mostly good, and some were raves. Goldie was pleased that critics noted her professional competency amid the group of singing-and-dancing amateurs. As weeks went by, the film was doing solid business.

The release, a couple of months later, of *The First Wives' Club* was a whole different story. The film received the kind of reviews that Goldie had not seen since *Private Benjamin*. But what really drove home the reality of Goldie's comeback was the tremendous box office, going over $100 million in record time—an achievement unheard of at a time when the prevailing Hollywood attitude continued to be that films starring women were box-office poison.

Goldie took an emotional time-out to revel in the glory, but as the late spring 1997 starting date drew closer, she threw herself even further into the process of making a movie, and that process hinged on her being fully prepared.

"I always saw this movie as being like building a house," she acknowledged. "First I had to get the plans right, then I had to get the foundation right. When I had those things together, then I had to go ahead and decorate it."

The early days of filming of *Hope* took place in Thompson, Texas, a small community south of Houston whose landscape, cramped roads, and small-town architecture mirrored the early 1960s feel *Hope* was trying to capture. When Goldie emerged from her trailer that first morning, her blond mane hanging limp and unmade, her eyes behind dark glasses, dressed in shorts, sleeveless shirt, and overall top, the signs were good. The sky was largely cloudless. The temperature was hot but not oppressively so. And Goldie was, well, Goldie.

She was laughing and chatting easily with her assistant director and cinematographer, setting up the particulars of the first shot of the day but doing it in a light, almost matter-of-fact and disarming way that had always been the hallmark of any Goldie Hawn project, no matter where she was in relation to the camera. On that first day, Goldie started with some relatively easy shots, the kinds of scenes designed to ease the cast, crew, and most importantly, the director into the filmmaking process: simple dialogue scenes with two people and crowd scenes. What became immediately evident was that Goldie did not need to be eased into the film.

181

Her creative instincts kicked in from the first take. She expertly framed shots, talked confidently with her actors, and was quick to consult with people when she had questions. In fact, that first day, according to crew members, she projected such a lack of ego and quiet control that the unspoken doubt as to whether Goldie was up to the challenge all but disappeared from the thoughts of the cast and crew.

The ice thus broken, *Hope* settled into an easygoing adventure that mirrored the philosophy of its director. And nobody blinked an eye when Goldie's perfectionism led to some rather unorthodox moments. Like the day when, while shooting a scene involving actress Mary Ellen Trainor, Goldie the director decided that the actress's hair did not look flyaway and ragged enough to convey the feel of the scene.

"It just doesn't look bad enough," said Hawn as she got up out of her director's chair and walked over to the actress. After a few moments of inspection, Goldie said "Let me see what I can do." Without a moment's thought to union regulations, Goldie led Trainor over to the director's chair, sat her down, and began to tease, spray, and comb the actress's locks. Finally, Goldie was satisfied with the disheveled job she had done and, laughing and giggling, resumed shooting.

Returning to Texas was, in a sense, like coming home again. More than one resident of Thompson and nearby Anderson remembered the last time Goldie had been in the state, making her dramatic breakthrough in *The Sugarland Express*. The irony was not lost on Hawn, who waxed philosophical over having once again returned to the Lone Star State to try something new.

Goldie's cool under pressure was contagious. Going into *Hope,* the collective feeling was that the fledgling director's debut would adhere largely to the script and that there would be little room for improvisation. What they quickly discovered was that because of her years in front of the camera Hawn had developed an instinct for giving actors their lead.

Veteran character actor J. T. Walsh, who played the almost laughably stereotypical role of Uncle Ray in the film, pointed out that Hawn had allowed him to do much more with what seemed a limited interpretation of the role. "The opportunity to play against the text is very rich," said Walsh during filming. "And Goldie's helping me that way. She's loosening me up. I do have very fixed notions about film acting as opposed to other kinds of acting, and Goldie is shaking them up a bit."

Christine Lahti, who last saw the acting and producing side of Goldie on *Swing Shift,* was not surprised at the flexibility she was being accorded by the first-time director. She described the working relationship as "teamwork" and praised Goldie for her fearlessness and willingness to try new things. "I tend to talk to Goldie a lot about character and the arc of the character. Maybe more so than I do with directors who aren't so knowledgeable about acting."

For her part, Hawn tended to downplay the degree of freedom she was providing her actors. "All I'm doing is bringing ideas to the actors and suggesting certain things to them. We're talking about the story and what we think should be done with it. There's a level of trust that has to happen for this to work. Everyone has a voice, and I listen to those voices."

It was mid-morning in the small, sleepy town of Anderson. Whereas normally little outside activity can be registered in the over-ninety degree heat and often monsoonlike conditions that envelop the town, Anderson is a beehive of activity. A small group of journalists have been invited down to observe the proceedings. Hundreds of local citizens, many armed with Instamatic cameras, have gathered outside the local courthouse. They are looking for the star of *Hope.* The real star.

Inside the courthouse, packed floor to ceiling with camera equipment, lights and the odd fan to combat the sweltering heat, Goldie is directing a tense courtroom scene. After finishing up a conversation with her cameraman on the logistics of an upcoming pan of the courtroom, she turns to face the viewing stands, packed with local extras. Dressed in cutoff blue jeans and a heat-friendly top and sporting an armful of gold bracelets, she is all smiles and good-natured banter, addressing her captive audience.

"Should I cue you?" she coos in giggly tones as she instructs the extras on how to react in the coming scene. "Does it feel better if I cue you?"

The extras roar with laughter. Loose and relaxed, the potentially problematic crowd scene now comes together in a relatively smooth handful of takes. Goldie thanks the extras for their cooperation before donning a pair of dark glasses and stepping out into the sunlight to the clatter of camera shutters and yells of recognition from the townspeople.

She stops momentarily to pose for pictures and sign autographs before gingerly making her way down the street to the nearby theater whose windows will be blown out as the result of a tense confrontation near the end of the film. She comes upon the special-effects people, who are already prepping the shot. Here Goldie is definitely out of her element, but she asks all the right questions about how to time the explosion so that the cameras aimed at the windows will capture the action. She steps behind a video monitor, checks the camera angles one more time, and yells action. The cameras roll for a few seconds before she yells to blow the windows. A loud boom echoes through the town as glass explodes outward in a shimmering rain.

"Cut!" yells Goldie. "Print it!"

Her own experience and feelings about growing up in the shadow of the bomb shelters came into play in *Hope*'s classroom scenes, where the bomb drills and everyday feelings about life in those times were reenacted. Goldie spoke to the child actors from her heart, sharing her own childhood experiences and feelings and giving her charges a personal glimpse into her youth. Those scenes, perhaps more than any others in *Hope*, rang the truest to the director, and those privy to the filming of them reported a lump in Goldie's throat and the occasional wiping of eyes.

Weather continued to be a constant and often inhospitable companion on the film. Muggy heat could change instantly to driving rain. Goldie, however, was rarely flustered, showcasing an innate flexibility to switch scenes, delegate authority, and to make sure not a second of *Hope*'s spartan schedule was wasted.

Despite her rookie status behind the camera, she was quick to join the ranks of filmmakers since time immemorial in bemoaning the lack of time and money that was preventing the extra take she would ideally like and the rushing from setup to setup that was the reality of Hawn's first directing job. "In many ways it's frustrating," she acknowledged. "I can't get in and do everything I want. I know that sometimes I've had to make a compromise in terms of a take or a shot. But basically it's been okay. It hasn't been that bad."

Goldie's ability to think fast and avoid panic was much in evidence on the second-to-last-day of filming. Goldie had just completed directing a complex five hours of fight sequences and was in her trailer fine-tuning another scene when there was a tentative knock on the door. It was her assistant director with some bad news. The can of film containing the much-needed fight footage had been accidentally exposed and was now useless. *Hope* was now in danger of going over budget and over schedule.

"Instead of panicking, I just went into a little thirty-second trance," recalled Hawn of her response to the crisis. She came out of the trance with the solution. That night, the fight sequence, in an admittedly modified form, was reshot. "In the end it was all that we needed," said Goldie.

Hope completed principal photography in late summer, on budget and on schedule. But the job was far from over. She would spend months in a darkened editing room, supervising the piecing together of thousands of feet of film into her vision. As she readied *Hope* for its initial showing to TNT executives and, shortly thereafter, the nation's most influential television critics, Goldie was feeling pretty good about her directing debut.

"It was wonderful directing this movie, because I got to leave my acting persona behind. That told me something about myself. It told me that if I never acted again, there is not a tear to be shed."

185

15

Glory

GOLDIE HAWN WAS IN A EUPHORIC STATE IN THE AFTERMATH OF her directing debut.

People close to her had seen the actress happy over the years. But it had always been a happiness in conflict with other emotions that ultimately kept her from feeling complete. In the wake of *Hope*, however, Goldie was hard-pressed to come up with anything negative.

"I like who I am," Hawn said of her current state of mind. "I look at love for whatever it is, and it's there to be lived to the fullest. The important thing is to remember to be happy for whatever it is that you get."

Her happiness, no doubt, had a lot to do with her family's flowering as well. Oliver had entered college and, while not settled yet on his life's work, was proving a bright, inquisitive man who had adopted much of his mother's laid-back attitudes toward life. Kate was showing that she inherited at least some of her mother's talent as she attempted to make her way as an actress. Wyatt, on the verge of entering high school, maintained the boyish charm and enthusiasm of both his parents. Kurt's career in action films had finally succeeded in putting him in the superstar category. Films like *Stargate*, *Executive Decision,* and *Breakdown* not only showed off his ability to be macho, with just a touch of vulnerability, but also proved that there was an immense audience for any film with Russell's name on the marquee.

Goldie carried on in a positive tone in her promotion of *Hope*. Interviewers asked the inevitable questions about the transition from actor to director, and she happily searched her memory to supply anecdotes. Much continued to be made of her personal life, her turning fifty, and the fact that she had reemerged in the 1990s as a bona-fide superstar. Rather than be annoyed by the personal inquiries, Goldie took the press interest as a positive sign.

Her appearance on *The Oprah Winfrey Show* quickly turned from the nuts and bolts of hyping the film to her philosophy of life. The exchange between Oprah and Goldie could have easily been dismissed as a blather fest by the terminally privileged. And while Winfrey's platitudes did come off as more than a little self-serving, Goldie's openness with her feelings came across as very real. "Sometimes you just hug your pillow at night and cry," she said. "But that doesn't mean that life is bad. It just means that's the way it is. Life is rich."

Hope aired on TNT in early October to generally favorable reviews. Goldie reveled in the praise for what critics perceived as her natural affinity for actors and storytelling and the prediction that there would be more of Goldie behind the camera in the future. Hawn was evenhanded in her assessment of a directing life. "If directing proves to be something that is part of my destiny, well, how great is that?"

But she immediately did an about-face, indicating that she did not want to drop acting altogether. "Acting is spontaneous. Directing requires that you be on in a certain way at all times. I could never give up being spontaneous."

Goldie Hawn was getting respect and, by association, being taken more seriously as a growing power behind the scenes. While always quick to take her calls, studio executives began responding more positively to her pitches for projects in which she was attached as actor, producer, or director.

Her continued attention to coproducing the remake of *The Out of Towners* had reached the serious stage and was scheduled to go before the cameras before the end of 1998. The years of pushing for a film treatment of the Broadway musical *Chicago* was finally bearing fruit. Director Herbert Ross had agreed to come aboard. Madonna had finally agreed to costar with Hawn, and the budget was being seriously reworked to accommodate the sudden interest of Rosie O'Donnell and John Travolta. Goldie was anxious to portray the pivotal role of Roxie Hart, the showgirl who confesses to murder to get publicity but winds up as an actual suspect.

As for other projects, Goldie was considering once again teaming up with Diane Keaton in a comedy called *Living Legends* and was continuing to try and get her private obsession, *Ashes to Ashes,* off the ground. Goldie had already agreed to direct and star in this very personal story, and a first-draft script was already being written by Jennifer Saunders. There were no immediate takers on *Ashes to Ashes,* but Goldie was confident that her pet project would eventually find a home. She was not about to sit still. "There are movies I want to make," she acknowledged of her full plate of projects. "There are things I want permission to have written. There are films I want to direct."

And the offers continued to come her way. Goldie's production arm, Cherry Alley, began putting the wheels in motion on the drama *The Cost of Living,* which chronicles the tale of a lonely woman who finally finds love with a gay man. The chemistry present on *The First Wives' Club* was also not lost on Hollywood. There was talk of reuniting Hawn, Midler, and Keaton in a send-up of the home-sale-of-cosmetics phenomenon entitled *Avon Ladies of the Amazon.* There were also reports of a "mystery script" being written that would likewise bring the *Wives'* actresses back together. Of the later project, Hawn would only say, "If it's good, we'll do it."

During this period, Goldie was enjoying a renewed joy in motherhood with her entire brood but was forming a particularly strong bond with her daughter, Kate. As she had with her own mother, Goldie had bonded with Kate at a very early age. Kate had been encouraged in all her endeavors and had the advantage of a mother who could impart advice born of experience of the best kind.

When Kate was thirteen and began showing an interest in boys, Goldie was there to caution her to "please don't go to the boys for your self-esteem. You've got to feel good about yourself."

And when her daughter decided, in her late teens, to pursue an acting career, Goldie was there with the stories of how rough acting could be and guided her through shortcuts and around potential pitfalls. But mixed in with the warnings was the encouragement to go for it. Even with nepotism rampant in Hollywood, Goldie refused to use her or Kurt's status to help Kate find work. She would constantly remind her daughter how special it would be if she got the work because of her own talent and not because of who she was related to.

Consequently, when Kate Hudson got her first acting jobs in 1997, (a small role in the TV series *Party of Five* and a lead role in the independent film *Ricochet River*), her mother was in seventh heaven.

It went without saying that Goldie's relationship with Kurt Russell was outlasting all expectations. The couple had recently celebrated their fifteenth year together and from all outward appearances were as much in love as the day they met. Their relationship, in fact, was so much of an oddity by virtue of its longevity that it often became the centerpiece of any interview involving either of them. Goldie, as always, was happy to point out the key to their happy ending.

"We stay together because we want to," she explained. "We're very much in love. I know how rare it is to stay together like we have done in this business for this amount of time. But doing our own things keeps a certain amount of mystery between us. And I love that. I never get undressed in front of Kurt. I just give him glimpses."

Russell, once again deflecting the marriage question, was philosophical in summing up his lengthy relationship with Hawn. "I enjoy my life with Goldie. I just think that there are people who are destined to meet and love each other forever. I feel that's the way Goldie and I are."

Hawn, at this late date, admits to having learned a lot from her previous relationships and from the strength that is her commitment to Russell. However, as if feeding the fantasy that nothing is forever, she does acknowledge that their union is essentially an open live-in relationship. "I know how rare it is to stay together this long and still be this much in love," she said. "He meets a lot of women, and I meet a lot of men. But so far nobody has come up for either of us that is better than what we already have."

Throughout 1997, Goldie continued to juggle personal and professional obligations. When they had the chance, Goldie and Kurt would steal away for some quiet time at their Canada retreat. She could often be found in her Cherry Alley offices, overlooking the ocean in Santa Monica, California, going over scripts, fielding production offers, and checking out any and all opportunities. Goldie, in the truest sense of the word, was Superwoman.

She danced around the notion that she was trying to have it all. But she did admit that a positive approach to life was allowing her to be, personally and professionally, many places at once. "Women can do four hundred things at once because we're equipped to do it. I don't know why. We're just able to juggle. We can be strong, we can be smart, and have an effect on society. But we can also be mothers and be warm and loving."

In her fifty-plus years, Goldie Hawn has seen it all—success, failure, heartbreak, love, and triumph. But as the millennium draws closer, Goldie is the first to acknowledge that there is much more to come.

"I know who I am, and I'm very proud of what I've accomplished. Now my focus is moving on to the next stage of my life. And that is about who I want to be at sixty, who I want to be at seventy, and who I want to be at eighty. I still have a lot to do."

Filmography

1968

The One and Only, Genuine, Original Family Band (Disney)
Producer: Walt Disney
Director: Michael O'Herilhy
Screenwriter: Lowell S. Hawley
Principal actors: Walter Brennan, Buddy Ebsen, Lesley Ann Warren,
  Kurt Russell, Goldie Hawn, Wally Cox, Richard Deacon, Janet
  Blair

1969

Cactus Flower (Columbia)
Producer: Mike Frankovich
Director: Gene Saks
Screenwriter: I. A. L. Diamond
Principal actors: Walter Matthau, Goldie Hawn, Ingrid Bergman,
  Jack Weston, Rick Lenz

1970

There's a Girl In My Soup (Columbia)
Producer: Mike Frankovich
Director: Roy Bolting
Screenwriter: Terence Frisby
Principal actors: Peter Sellers, Goldie Hawn, Tony Britton, Nicky
  Henson, Diana Dors, Nicola Pagett, Christopher Cazenove

1972

$ (Dollars) (Columbia)
Producer: Mike Frankovich
Director: Richard Brooks
Screenwriter: Richard Brooks
Principal actors: Warren Beatty, Goldie Hawn, Gert Fröbe, Scott
    Brady, Robert Webber

Butterflies Are Free (Columbia)
Producer: Mike Frankovich
Director: Milton Katselas
Screenwriter: Leonard Gershe
Principal actors: Goldie Hawn, Edward Albert, Eileen Heckart,
    Michael Glaser

1974

The Girl From Petrovka (Universal)
Producers: Richard Zanuck, David Brown
Director: Robert Ellis Miller
Screenwriters: Allan Scott, Chris Bryant
Principal actors: Goldie Hawn, Hal Holbrook, Anthony Hopkins.

The Sugarland Express (Universal)
Producers: Richard Zanuck, David Brown
Director: Steven Spielberg
Screenwriters: Hal Barwood, Matthew Robbins
Principal actors: Goldie Hawn, Ben Johnson, Michael Sacks, William
    Atherton

1975

Shampoo (Columbia)
Producer: Warren Beatty
Director: Hal Ashby
Screenwriters: Warren Beatty, Robert Towne
Principal actors: Warren Beatty, Julie Christie, Goldie Hawn, Jack

Warden, Lee Grant, Tony Bill, Carrie Fisher, William Castle, Howard Hessman

1976

The Duchess and the Dirtwater Fox (Twentieth Century–Fox)
Producer: Melvin Frank
Director: Melvin Frank
Screenwriters: Melvin Frank, Barry Sandler
Principal actors: George Segal, Goldie Hawn, Conrad Janis, Thayer David

1978

Foul Play (Paramount)
Producers: Thomas L. Miller, Edward K. Milkis
Director: Colin Higgins
Screenwriter: Colin Higgins
Principal actors: Goldie Hawn, Chevy Chase, Dudley Moore, Burgess Meredith, Billy Barty, Rachel Roberts, Eugene Roche, Brian Dennehy, Chuck McCann, Bruce Solomon

1979

Lovers and Liars, a.k.a. *Travels With Anita* (New Line)
Producer: Albert Grimaldi
Director: Mario Monicelli
Screenwriters: Leo Benevenuti, Pietro De Bernardi, Tullio Pinelli, Paul Zimmerman
Principal actors: Goldie Hawn, Giancarlo Giannini, Laura Betti

1980

Private Benjamin (Warner Bros.)
Producers: Goldie Hawn, Nancy Meyers, Charles Shyer, Harvey Miller
Director: Howard Zieff
Screenwriters: Nancy Meyers, Charles Shyer, Harvey Miller

Principal actors: Goldie Hawn, Eileen Brennan, Albert Brooks, Robert Webber, Armand Assante, Barbara Barrie, Mary Kay Place, Sally Kirkland, Craig T. Nelson, Harry Dean Stanton, Sam Wanamaker

Seems Like Old Times (Columbia)
Producer: Ray Stark
Director: Jay Sandrich
Screenwriter: Neil Simon
Principal actors: Goldie Hawn, Chevy Chase, Charles Grodin, Robert Guillaume, Harold Gould, George Grizzard, T. K. Carter

1982

Best Friends (Warner Bros.)
Producers: Joe Wizan, Norman Jewison
Director: Norman Jewison
Screenwriters: Valerie Curtin, Barry Levinson
Principal actors: Goldie Hawn, Burt Reynolds, Jessica Tandy, Barnard Hughes, Audra Lindley, Keenan Wynn, Ron Silver

1984

Protocol (Warner Bros.)
Producer: Anthea Sylbert
Director: Herbert Ross
Screenwriter: Buck Henry
Principal actors: Goldie Hawn, Chris Sarandon, Andre Gregory, Cliff De Young, Ed Begley Jr., Gail Strickland, Richard Romanus, Keith Szarabajka, James Staley, Kenneth Mars, Kenneth McMillian, Archie Hahn, Amanda Bearse

Swing Shift (Warner Bros.)
Producers: Goldie Hawn, Anthea Sylbert, Jerry Bick
Director: Jonathan Demme
Screenwriters: Rob Morton a.k.a. Rob Nyswaner, Bo Goldman, Nancy Dowd

Principal actors: Goldie Hawn, Kurt Russell, Ed Harris, Christine Lahti, Holly Hunter, Chris Lemmon, Belinda Carlisle, Fred Ward, Roger Corman, Lisa Pelikan

1986

Wildcats (Warner Bros.)
Producer: Anthea Sylbert
Director: Michael Ritchie
Screenwriter: Ezra Sacks
Principal actors: Goldie Hawn, James Keach, Swoosie Kurtz, Bruce McGill, M. Emmet Walsh

1987

Overboard (M-G-M)
Producers: Alexandra Rose, Anthea Sylbert
Director: Garry Marshall
Screenwriter: Leslie Dixon
Principal actors: Goldie Hawn, Kurt Russell, Katherine Helmond, Roddy McDowall, Edward Herrmann

1990

Bird on a Wire (Universal)
Producer: Ron Cohen
Director: John Badham
Screenwriters: David Seltzer, Louis Venosta, Eric Lerner
Principal actors: Mel Gibson, Goldie Hawn, David Carradine, Bill Duke, Stephen Tobolowsky

1991

Deceived (Touchstone)
Producers: Michael Finnell, Wendy Dozoretz, Ellen Collett
Director: Damian Harris
Screenwriters: Mary Agnes Donoghue, Derek Saunders
Principal actors: Goldie Hawn, John Heard, Ashley Peldon

1992

Crisscross (M-G-M)
Producers: Goldie Hawn, Anthea Sylbert
Director: Chris Menges
Screenwriter: Scott Sommer
Principal actors: Goldie Hawn, David Arnott, Arliss Howard, James Gammon, Keith Carradine, J. C. Quinn

HouseSitter
Producer: Brian Grazer
Director: Frank Oz
Screenwriter: Mark Stein
Principal actors: Goldie Hawn, Steve Martin, Dana Delany, Julie Harris, Donald Moffat, Peter MacNicol, Richard B. Shull, Laurel Cronin, Christopher Durang

Death Becomes Her (Universal)
Producers: Robert Zemeckis, Steven Starkey
Director: Robert Zemeckis
Screenwriters: Martin Donovon, David Koepp
Principal actors: Meryl Streep, Goldie Hawn, Bruce Willis, Isabella Rossellini, Ian Ogilvy, Adam Storke, Nancy Fish, Alaina Reed Hall, Michelle Johnson, Mimi Kennedy, Jonathan Silverman, Fabio, Sydney Pollack

1996

Everybody Says I Love You (Miramax)
Producer: Woody Allen
Director: Woody Allen
Screenwriter: Woody Allen

Principal actors: Woody Allen, Goldie Hawn, Julia Roberts, Alan Alda, Edward Norton, Drew Barrymore

The First Wives' Club (Paramount)
Producer: Scott Rudin
Director: Hugh Wilson
Screenwriter: Paul Rudnick
Principal actors: Goldie Hawn, Bette Midler, Diane Keaton, Elizabeth Berkley, John Stewart

Sources

The following books helped pave the way for this most up-to-date chronicle on Goldie Hawn's life: *Goldie* by Peter Haining and *Solid Goldie* by Connie Burman, which brought Goldie from birth to Private Benjamin. *Wake Me When It's Funny* by Lori Marshall, *Spielberg* by Philip M. Taylor, *My Life* by Burt Reynolds, *Stephen Spielberg* by Joseph McBride, *Warren Beatty and Desert Eyes* by David Thomson, *Walther Matthau* by Alan Hunter, *You'll Never Eat Lunch in This Town Again* by Julia Phillips, *Lethal Hero: The Mel Gibson Story* by Roland Perry, *Current Biography, Leonard Maltin's Movie and Video Guide, Video Hound's Golden Retriever and Total Television* by Alex McNeil.

Many thanks to the following magazines for the vital information they revealed: *People, Marquee, McCalls, Newsweek, Life, Entertainment, US, Ladies Home Journal, Cosmopolitan, Elle, Premiere, Film Comment, Glamor, Esquire, BAM, Fame, Interview, Vanity Fair, Good Housekeeping, Premiere, W, Macleans, International Photographer, Starlog, Rolling Stone, Redbook, Vogue, Working Woman, Harpers Bazaar, TV Guide, Saturday Evening Post, Playboy, New Dawn, West, Parade, TV Times, Playgirl* and *New Choices.*

The following newspapers provided valuable information: *Los Angeles Times, Los Angeles Herald Examiner, New York Times, Hollywood Reporter, Variety, Star, Los Angeles Daily News, New York Daily News, Long Beach Press Telegram, Christian Science Monitor, Village View* and *Chicago Tribune.*

Pure Goldie quite simply tells the tale. The next chapter in Goldie Hawn's life, and the inevitable stories that only Goldie herself can tell, remains to be written.

Index

205